Anne R. Gladstone Bennett, Albert Tesniere

The Eucharistic Christ Reflections

and considerations on the blessed sacrament

Anne R. Gladstone Bennett, Albert Tesniere

The Eucharistic Christ Reflections
and considerations on the blessed sacrament

ISBN/EAN: 9783337361105

Printed in Europe, USA, Canada, Australia, Japan

Cover: Foto ©Lupo / pixelio.de

More available books at **www.hansebooks.com**

The Eucharistic Christ.

Reflections and Considerations on the Blessed Sacrament.

BY

REV. A. TESNIÈRE,

Priest of the Congregation of the Blessed Sacrament.

TRANSLATED BY

MRS. ANNE R. BENNETT-GLADSTONE

WITH A PREFACE BY

REV. D. J. McMAHON, D.D.,

General Director for the United States of the Apostolic Union of Secular Priests.

NEW YORK, CINCINNATI, CHICAGO:

BENZIGER BROTHERS,

Printers to the Holy Apostolic See.

1897

Nihil Obstat.

                     J. McMahon, D.D.,
                               Censor Deputatus.

Imprimatur.

                ✠ MICHAEL AUGUSTINE,
                             Archbishop of New York.

NEW YORK, June 24, 1897.

Preface.

"AT the sight of the love of Jesus in His adorable Sacrament, of the isolation in which He is left, of the little piety and great indifference among so many Christians, and of the ever-increasing impiety of the age; at the view of the extended and pressing wants of the Church I have said, Why should there not be some men whose mission would be to pray perpetually at the feet of Jesus Christ in the Ever-Blessed Sacrament?"

It was thus that the Rev. Fr. Eymard, after four years of prayer and preparation, exposed to Pope Pius IX. his plan of forming the Society of Priests of the Blessed Sacrament. He explained further the various duties which the society could fulfil usefully, and which had not that systematic care which was becoming to them.

Pius IX. replied with earnestness to the petition, saying, "I am convinced that this thought comes from God. The Church has need of it. Let every means be taken to spread the knowledge of the Holy Eucharist."

For nearly twenty years Fr. Eymard had labored as a Marist, and by reason of the positions which he held as provincial and director he was prepared for the arduous duty of forming a new community. He had tried every breach, had tested every sign before he would give any heed to the project which seemed, however, to grow more imperative when he would endeavor to put it aside. When he finally determined, after five years of careful thought and prayer, to take the step, he formulated his plan and proposed it almost as completely as it is found to-day. It comprises the Society of the Blessed Sacrament, a community of priests whose whole duty is to keep perpetual adoration in their convent and to preach the Blessed Sacrament abroad. "You do not become a member of this Society of the Blessed Sacrament," said the venerated founder to his novices, "in order to become virtuous; nor do you enter to amass a greater sum of merit and a higher degree of glory in heaven. No; for you yourself would be the first object of your service. You have entered solely to immolate your personality to the service of Jesus Christ and to procure for Him the greatest possible glory by the homage of a love which will reach as readily to the heroism of sacrifice as it will to the simplest and most natural act of your duty. The praise, the merit will go to Jesus, your Master; the soldier gains the victory and dies; the king alone triumphs and obtains its glory."

This spirit of complete renunciation was constantly inculcated in order that his priests might lead lives with no other thought than to make known the love of the Prisoner of the tabernacle. That this great end might be more widely gained he formed the Confraternity of the Priest Adorers. These have the duty of spending at least an hour weekly in adoration before the Blessed Sacrament, whence they might draw that fervor which would be manifested in their works of zeal. That this devotion towards the Holy Eucharist might be extended, he planned the Aggregation of Lay-Adorers, whose members spend one hour monthly in adoration. Besides this personal service, these are generally to be attached to some of the various works which centre in the Blessed Sacrament, as the tabernacle and altar societies, etc.

Fr. Eymard died in 1868, and in the thirty years which have since passed, his work has developed beyond the highest expectation of its founder. The society has been established in very many dioceses and numbers its members among the hundreds. The Confraternity of Priest Adorers has struck a responsive chord in the hearts of the devoted friends of the Eucharistic Lord. Its members number already fifty thousand, of which about three thousand are in the United States. The influence of the work among priests is extended far beyond this number of members, for very many have renewed good wishes and resolves in their devotion through the knowledge which the existence of this confraternity imparts. Not all take the word of entering organizations for works of purely personal piety, but they are encouraged and stimulated in their individual lines by the zeal which the organizations must show forth.

In the interest of this confraternity many works have been published in French by the members of the society. The present, "The Eucharistic Christ," is the first that has been put into English dress in the hope that its reflections and pious thoughts may find favor among the American members of the confraternity.

The establishment of this society and confraternity at this period in the Church's history seems, indeed, singular, for the Blessed Sacrament has ever been the centre of all worship in the Church. To awaken, however, to vivify and increase the faith and love of Catholics in this august mystery is surely a becoming duty in our age.

If we view the subject historically we shall see that the establishment of the Blessed Sacrament as a special devotion belongs to that doctrinal development of which every age gives us examples. It seems like a grade in that progress towards the perfection of our devotion.

The Blessed Sacrament first presents itself to our view

under the awful mystery of the Mass. In the Church has this sacrifice been at all times a necessity, and we cannot consider it as an act of devotion, since it pertains to the essence of the religion. There never was a time when attendance at Sunday Mass was not obligatory. The commandment of the Church to hear Mass on Sunday is the formulation in words of an obligation which is sunk deep in the heart and conscience of Christendom. Even though for a time it seemed to be obscured, Fr. Bridgett, in his work on the "Devotion to the Blessed Sacrament in England," shows how universal was the practice and how important it was considered at all times centuries before it was taught in the Catechism. Holy communion, the second aspect of the Holy Eucharist, was at first deemed a necessity for all attendants at Mass. As late as the fourth century a Council of Antioch, under Pope Julius, pronounced censures against those who heard Mass and did not communicate thereat. This decree was based upon the Apostolical Constitutions. To the hermits and Cenobites this law was equally applicable. In the course of time custom limited the obligation to the Sunday Mass. Bishops and rulers urged this duty, but the inroads of the barbarians and their subsequent conversion brought more and more the spirit of relaxation to the piety and recollection demanded for the frequent reception of this adorable mystery. For it was difficult to awaken at once these "rude children of the forest to the proper spirit of devotion." From the ninth to the thirteenth century, in this glorious period of the Crusades, in these ages of faith, strange is it to find that communions were rare among the faithful. There are some particular cases of frequent communion in saintly lives at this as at other epochs. But when we find the Religious Orders lax in this saintly duty, what can be expected of the faithful living in the world ? Thus, Dalgairns, in "The Holy Communion," from which these facts are principally culled, shows that "in the only genuine English Order that ever was established, called the Gilbertins—after the founder, St. Gilbert, contemporary of St. Thomas à Becket—the Lay-Brothers communicated only eight times a year." Some decades later we have the seraphic St. Francis allowing one Mass daily in each convent, no matter how numerous the priests might be therein. In the Order of the Poor Clares, the Sisters were permitted by rule to receive communion only six times a year. The novices of the Benedictine Order were much more restrained, since they were limited to three times a year. The Council of Vienna for these last, as the Council of Trent for the Poor Clares, ordained that communion should be received at least once a month.

It may, indeed, be that there were less dangers for faith or morals in those days, and hence there was less need of the frequent reception of the saving power of holy communion ; but to our eyes the command of the Lateran Council to communicate at least once a year appears to have been framed none too soon. From that time until our own time, except for a short period under Jansenistic influence, the present discipline in relation to the frequency of reception has prevailed in the Church. Neither the Mass nor communion can be considered as a special devotion, since they are duties from which an obligation arises that must receive attention. They are necessary parts of our Christian life, and have been duties from the beginning. Upon these two aspects of the Blessed Sacrament all saintly piety expended itself until the thirteenth century. The development of Christian truth and the efflorescence of Catholic devotion seem in a measure to have been arrested from the sixth until the twelfth century, as the Church had then her wars with rulers and her struggles with the barbarians. It was the Berengarian heresy of the latter century which brought into clearer view the doctrine and devotion of the Blessed Sacrament. Immediately thereafter followed the decree of the Lateran Council about Paschal communion, etc., which was reduced to practice among the faithful through the preaching of the saints who then adorned the Church, but principally through the devotion kindled by the institution of the Feast of Corpus Christi.

The procession of the Blessed Sacrament, which soon became the feature of this feast, was introduced shortly after its institution to give the most solemn honor to our Eucharistic Lord as an answer to the heretical opinions of Berengarius. The feast for the universal Church was approved by Urban IV. in 1264, and at his suggestion the Angelic Doctor wrote the Office. The observance did not, however, become general for seventy years after this. The Blessed Sacrament was borne about in procession in the sacred pyx, but was not, as now, exposed to the view of the faithful.

For over two hundred years it was the sole public devotion to the Blessed Sacrament beyond the Mass and communion, and it doubtless aided to confirm and strengthen the faith of the people, which was tried by the failure of the Crusades and the Western schism.

From this procession, when the Council of Trent had finished its course, there arose the Devotion of the Forty Hours. Within a few years after its first introduction, whether that be attributed to St. Charles and the Friar Joseph at Milan, or to the Jesuits in Macerata, the devotion was established in the churches of Rome, and thence spread slowly to the Catholic world. The devotion of the Benediction of the Blessed Sacrament came in later. It was by slow steps that the Blessed Sacrament became exposed to the view of the faithful, and that monstrances were made in the shape that now obtains. The next development in the devotion of the Blessed Sacrament was that of visiting Our Lord dwelling in the tabernacle. Doubtless at all times in the history of the Church there were souls who would occasionally perform this sacred duty. We can the more readily believe it of those early days of persecution, when the faithful brought home with them the Blessed Sacrament, that they might communicate themselves on the morrow.

In the quiet of their own homes they must have given free rein to their hearts' impulses of adoration and love towards the Eucharistic Lord. So, too, from the various private revelations do we learn that visits to the Blessed Sacrament were common in the religious houses, but the practice has become general among the faithful only as a very late development.

Finally, from this devotion of visiting the Blessed Sacrament arose in a short time the practice of perpetual adoration of the Blessed Sacrament. Perpetual adoration of some kind was ever in the Church from the earliest days, when the monks spent most of their time in their chapels; but this devotion as applied to the Blessed Sacrament was instituted about 1660 in France by the Sisters of the Annunciation. The number of religious communities of Sisters who are now devoted to this work is very large, and are to be found in almost every Order. The Benedictines, the Dominicans, and the Franciscans, however, bear the palm. The practice of perpetual adoration is not confined to the nuns of the contemplative life, for some who are most actively engaged have adopted it also. A distinction might here be made between those devoted to perpetual adoration and to perpetual exposition, but it is aside from our present purpose. It was reserved to Fr. Eymard, in our day, to establish a society of priests for this same object and to open to all priests a participation in this duty and in its rewards.

The one great object of all these devotions to the Blessed Sacrament—procession, Forty Hours, Benediction, visits, and perpetual adoration—is to deepen our love and intensify our reparation, and thus prepare ourselves for a more worthy reception of the graces of the Holy Eucharist.

Each age has its own character impressed upon it, and Providence so disposes the course of nature that the predominating feature will in the end make itself known and felt. Into the groove which will be formed men's minds and wills will be turned and the work of the age will unconscionably be directed to the progress which is the result. The character is the product of the work which has, under God's watchful care, received its turn and course from the efforts of some man living in the age. He may be comparatively unknown, he may have only some meagre ends to gain, but he has opened the spring at the opportune moment, and the age becomes his debtor for its name and character. This is true not only for the chief or principal feature of an age, but is as well for those eddies and currents that bear onward a goodly portion of the human race.

In our time there are a large number of devotions which occupy the minds of pious Christians. Religious societies and confraternities for special objects are bidding for the attention and the affection of the faithful. They all aim at bringing us nearer to God through the practice of various virtues, and must be commended for their zeal and earnestness. From every point of his life, work, and character different devotional practices would enter to win man's allegiance to his Maker. But for the Blessed Sacrament, the source and centre of Christian life, there was no special society, with the exception of the few convents for nuns in which perpetual adoration had been established. The devotion to the Sacred Heart, in urging the need of reparation for sacrilegious communions, with its other purposes, comes near to it. Many religious foundations looked to this same end as well. But there was no general society having only the Blessed Sacrament in view until the time of Fr. Eymard.

The Blessed Sacrament had been a special devotion among many of the saints and pious people in all times, for it can be viewed as an essential part of the Christian religion and as the object of a special and particular devotion. All Catholics must render their meed of adoration in the Mass, in holy communion, and therein is it of strict and severe obligation, an essential part of Christian duty. But the special devotion extends to that mindful observance and active memory of the adorable presence of our divine Lord. It is that constant thought and earnest wish to express our love and adoration and to bow down in humble prayer before the tabernacle. It finds expression in the many sources which an intense love will ever frame and fashion.

God has shown His approval of this special devotion in the past by giving to many pious souls the miraculous power of ever discerning His presence even by the senses. Some could tell the consecrated from the unconsecrated Host by the taste; others by the odor; others by the mere presence, as Louise Lateau. To others Our Lord has communicated Himself in miraculous ways, as going from the priest's hand to St. Catharine of Sienna and Blessed Imelda, or piercing through the breast of St. Juliana Falconieri.

The establishment and diffusion of this special devotion at this time seems, indeed, to accord with the canons of God's dealings with man. In the sixth decade of this century, just when Darwin had won great favor in the English world by his materialistic work ; when Büchner had deepened the irreligious channel of Vogt in German minds ; when the enthusiasm of the new and seemingly convincing evidence had placed infidelity on a strong basis of science—then it was that Fr. Eymard brought forth this devotion to the Blessed Sacrament by the establishment, one after the other, of his religious body, the Association of Priest-Adorers, and the Aggregation of Lay-Adorers.

The Lord seems to delight in paradoxes in the establishment of His reign among men. He would seem to choose the most unpropitious time and manner for the accomplishment of His purposes. But " the Lord hath regard to the prayer of the humble" (Ps. ci. 18), and when the intellectual world seemed in opposition "He looked forth from His high sanctuary . . . upon the earth," and He determines that " the people shall be created who will praise the Lord." He will " choose the weak to confound the strong" (1 Cor. i. 27), and just as " He changeth times and ages, giving wisdom to the wise and knowledge to them that have understanding" (Dan. ii. 21) for the end He would obtain ; so at the time when the world was trusting only to matter does He introduce this special devotion to the Blessed Sacrament, which is so far removed from that which deals with the purely material. May we not also say that the Spirit of the Blessed Sacrament which Father Faber so beautifully shows to be the Spirit of the Holy Infancy, namely, simplicity and hidden life, is directly opposed to the spirit of the age, ever desirous of proclaiming and extolling its various beneficent deeds ?

Father Olier, the founder of the Sulpitians, had the thought in the seventeenth century of establishing a body of priests who would be wholly employed in spreading the devotion to the Blessed Sacrament; but the Lord in His all-wise counsel reserved it to the year when it would seem a consequence of the proclamation of the dogma of the Immaculate Conception.

It is, indeed, needed that great and constant attention should be given to Our Lord's presence. For eighteen centuries He has been upon our altars, and how much like a prison has His tabernacle oftentimes seemed! What prophet could have foretold that He would thus dwell among men and that He would be treated as if He were not, as if it were painful to remain in His presence?

As the animals of old crowded around Adam in the Garden of Eden, to honor him as their master, should not all men also crowd around, sing out their praise, and seek the benediction of their Lord and Master on every occasion? We would have thought that God's presence in His creation would have ever won man's attention; that the Church where He welcomes us would seemingly be the one place where we should love to come, where, indeed, we would ever find our home. But "He came unto His own and His own received Him not." There was very frequently only solitude and cheerlessness for Him. The light of the sanctuary lamp is oft the only active attendant that is destined to acknowledge His presence. He has become no company to His creatures, and thus is He left to solitude. Man has care and esteem of all in this world but the Creator of the world. True, all earnest members of the Church attended the weekly Mass and oft found solace in holy communion, but the visit, the special devotion to the Blessed Sacrament, the active, constant memory of His presence, seemed a matter which suited only the cloister and religious habit. As we enter into the thought of God's dealing with men, does there not seem to be a constant round of failure? It appears written upon all His enterprises. God's gifts are without repentance, and, having once given us His presence on earth, He cannot withdraw it forever. His sacramental presence is to be ever with us until the veil of Mercy shall be turned to that of Justice, and our deeds shall receive from Him their rightful recompense. We would have thought that every precaution would be taken in order that He should be always acknowledged in the sacrament of His love. But when we recount His dealings with His creation, how strange becomes this frequent appearance of failure!

The creation of the angels was a failure, for one-third fell and set up a hostile activity against His saving will. The Garden of Eden was a failure, bringing upon us the results of the disastrous fall of Adam and Eve. So, too, was the Saviour's mission, for His lifework was confined to a small part of northern Africa, and won only a few followers to His doctrines. Nor did He seem to aim any higher, for He preaches so that His meaning is oft concealed in figures and parables; He worked miracles, but would have them unnoticed, and closes His life by condemnation as a criminal. "Verily," might we say with Isaias, "Thou art a God that hidest Thyself, a hidden God, the God of Israel, the Saviour." The great miracle of the Resurrection which was the corner-stone for credence in Him was not revealed to all, but to a chosen few. Retirement, defeat before the advance of man seems ever the way of the Lord, and did not our faith uphold us, we should be severely tried at this constant recession. So, too, in His dealings with man in this sacrament of faith. For not only is there absolute neglect and carelessness of His presence, but there is from His enemies open outrage and scandalous abuse, which in all meekness He suffers without complaint.

The more, however, we sink into the study of God's dealings in our regard it will be apparent that He discloses Himself in hiding. For the characteristics of His withdrawal show us that it is godlike. Its constant secrecy, its helplessness, joined to its ignominy and defeat, show that it is more than human, and the after-success will not then surprise us.

God desires that He shall be sought diligently—for His many-sided perfections, the magnificence of His attributes would not be appreciated were they ever before us. He is hidden behind the wonderful effects of His creation, though their beauty, their wisdom, and their power ravish us by their grandeur. So, too, in the wonderful works for our supernatural destiny He has evidenced His handiwork, though the beauty and splendor of His appearance are denied us.

"Why," asks Fenelon, "has God established His general laws? It is to hide, under the veil of the regulated and uniform cause of nature, His perpetual operation from the eyes of proud and corrupt men, while, on the other hand, He gives to pure and docile souls something which they may admire in all His works."

Ofttimes is it only after reflection upon the reception of some favors that, like the disciples of Emmaus, we recognize the giver. Faith, hope, and charity here below must be exercised in seeking after Him, in pursuing the path that leads to the brightness of eternal bliss; but how many of His creatures truly pursue it? "There would seem to be some repulsion, some centrifugal force in Him who is the centre of minds, and souls, and lives."

So indeed is it with our dear Lord in the Blessed Sacrament; for the repulsion that generates "this is a hard saying, and who can believe it?" the negligence that cares not for His presence, and the indifference that thinks not of this mystery—all show the want of true esteem of a very large number for this greatest gift of God. While the Lord, on His part, seems not to draw or hold the attention to the tabernacle's Dweller.

It would seem to be the general tenor of the effect of His presence to treat us as we treat Him. For the careless and indifferent there seems no stirring of His affection except on rare occasions; but for the devout the rays of His love so warm and brighten their hearts as to urge them to greater love. To some souls it is given to make amends for man's frequent forgetfulness of God, and to none should it be so strict a duty as to the members of that society whose aim is to diffuse and extend the love of Our Lord. That this love may be deepened and broadened, frequent serious meditation must be made upon the mystery, that thus we may be able to unfold more securely the riches of God's goodness and charity.

No depth in creation is so shrouded in impenetrable secrecy as Our Lord's presence under the consecrated Host. The eye of the greatest saint to whom the glories of heaven have been revealed knows not the manner of His presence. The brightest saint in the vaults of the blessed, enriched with the light of glory through which the beatific vision is viewed, endowed with the aureoles of the virgin and martyr, added to the marks of the apostle and confessor, cannot discern the depths of this mystery in itself. Even the angels to whom in a special manner the care of the Blessed Sacrament is commissioned know it not, while the devils simply believe and tremble, for their knowledge does not extend so far. Nor can we ever become familiarized with it on account of the mysteries it contains.

There are miracles and mysteries as well in the operations of Our Lord in the Eucharist; for in the Blessed Sacrament we have the same Christ who " dying once, dies now no more." He is living and active. There is His divinity, His soul, and His body, and to each must be ascribed the operations consonant with His sacramental presence. His heart is there touched by our earnest prayer; His intellect also, not alone by the view which the beatific vision and infused science grants, but also by the operations of His senses, as many worthy theologians teach, thus stretching out to this realm of wonderful mystery the axiom, "*Nihil in intellectu nisi prius fuerit in sensu.*"

Here is a world of activity and of grandeur, and the thirst for knowledge which is natural to the children of Adam must extend into it in order that our love and devotion to the Lord may become intensified. The pious soul loves to dwell upon this aspect of our Saviour's presence, for it brings Him so near to us; we regard Him as looking down upon us with His own eyes as if in His visible corporal presence, and through our own sensibility our hearts open out to Him with all the effulgence and devotion of which they are capable.

"All do not take this word" of deep and constant devotion; but those who are dedicated to the service of the altar have indeed a duty to extend the sway of this incomparable gift among the faithful, and in a special manner for the priest-adorers of the Eucharistic League does it become a loved labor.

"We should be," says Fr. Faber, "all for Jesus, if Jesus is our all. The Blessed Sacrament should be to us the single overpowering fact of the world. Our hands hold Him; our words make Him; our tongue rests Him; our body compasses Him; our soul feels Him; our flesh feeds upon Him—Him, the Infinite, the Incomprehensible, the Immense, the Eternal. Must not all life be looked at in this light, just as the whole Church lies in this light and has no other? Our whole being thus resolves itself into one double duty, one while praise, and another while reparation to this Most Holy Sacrament."

In the spiritual unseen world the angelic thrones, under the leadership of the Archangel Michael, are ever in constant attendance upon the Blessed Sacrament, but in the visible world their place is taken by the priest, and especially the priest-adorer, since he has bound himself thereto in a particular manner. Close indeed is the priest to the Lord as His minister and His priest. Great, too, should be His knowledge and love of this sublime mystery.

"Our whole life as priests," says again Fr. Faber, "resolves itself into duties and ceremonies with regard to it. To that end are we deputed. We are taken out of the world and set apart. The mark of Jesus Christ is put upon us, and the spirit of the world, and the ways of the world, and the allowable things even of the world are to us what they are not to others. We have to enter the Holy of Holies daily in one way or another. We have to handle God, and to be ready at all moments to wait upon and carry about and administer the infinite substantial purity of the Most High. An invisible character has been sculptured upon our soul by the chisel of the Holy Ghost, that we may be the property of the Blessed Sacrament forever. Our hands have been anointed to touch Jesus. Even He Himself in the holy oil of Extreme Unction shrinks from the spot where that other greater unction went before. Oh! what are we and what should we be? Mary drew the Eternal Word down from heaven once, while we draw Him daily. She bore Him in her arms till He grew beyond it; but with us His sacred infancy is prolonged throughout our lives. Can we look into our Mother's face and tell her we are in this way greater than she and then not think of the holiness our dread office requires? To Jesus Himself we are Mary, and Joseph, and the apostles, and the evangelists, and if His dear sacrament requires it the company of martyrs also; while to the people we are as Jesus Himself. With us priests self-preservation is but the second law of our nature; the preservation of the Blessed Sacrament is our first. Oh, how happy would the slow martyrdom of our unworldly lives be did we but strive after sacerdotal holiness! If we attract the Blessed Sacrament even so far off as the throne of God in heaven, ought we not to feel His corresponding affection in our hearts? The attraction of the Holy Eucharist is our vocation, our ecclesiastical spirit, our sanctity, our joy."

That our knowledge of this great mystery may be increased, and that our love and esteem may be deepened until it shall absorb our whole being, this work of "The Eucharistic Christ" is presented to the clients of the Blessed Sacrament. In its English dress it is the first work which is offered specially to the American members of the Priests' Eucharistic League. It has been written *con amore* by one of the society which Fr. Eymard founded; and the writer shows that he has well imbibed the spirit of that devoted friend of the Blessed Sacrament.

In a series of meditations which are searching in their theological acumen there are joined reflections which will appeal to the devotion of all. There is solidity in the explanations while there is poetry in the touching applications.

Whatever will extend the glory of the eucharistic reign of Our Saviour; whatever will enliven our faith and love for this hidden God, dwelling ever among us, almost as if He were not; whatever will increase the devotion of visiting Our Lord prisoned in the tabernacle will surely be in accord with the devotional development of this sublime mystery and will meet with a hearty response from every loyal priest. To promote these ends has been the purpose of the writer of this book, and we are sure that the weekly hour of Adoration will be very profitably engaged by meditating upon any of the subjects which are here prepared. They are calculated to win us to serious reflection and frequent thought and mention of the Blessed Sacrament.

Commencing thus first with himself, the priest will spread abroad more earnestly " the fire that came to devour the earth."

D. J. McMahon.

Feast of Corpus Christi, 1897.

Contents.

	PAGE
PREFACE,	1
INTRODUCTION.—PRACTICAL CONSIDERATIONS ON THE ADORATION OF THE MOST HOLY SACRAMENT,	9

THE INSTITUTION OF THE EUCHARIST.

THE FACT,	41
THE MASTERPIECE OF GOD,	49
THE PRIEST,	57
THE SACRIFICE,	65

THE EUCHARIST A MEMORIAL OF THE PASSION,	80
THE MOST HOLY BODY OF JESUS,	94
THE PRECIOUS BLOOD,	100
THE HEART OF JESUS IN THE EUCHARIST,	110
THE FIVE WOUNDS,	125
THE EUCHARISTIC STATE,	148
THE DIFFUSION OF THE EUCHARIST: EVERYWHERE!	161
THE PERPETUITY OF THE EUCHARIST: ALWAYS!	169
THE UNIVERSALITY OF THE EUCHARIST: TO ALL!	178

Introduction.

Practical Considerations upon the Adoration of the Most Holy Sacrament.

I. THE OBJECT AND THE END OF THE ADORATION.

In order rightly to understand the nature of a virtue, the duties which it imposes, the acts which it ought to inspire, and the spirit in which they ought to be accomplished, it is necessary to understand as clearly as possible its object and its end.

What, then, is the object, what is the aim of the adoration of the Most Blessed Sacrament, the most excellent act of all the virtue of religion?

This is what we desire to point out in a simple and practical manner for the greatest utility of all those souls who, by the influence of God's grace, have enrolled themselves in our various eucharistic associations, where the adoration of the Most Holy Sacrament is the principal object. The spiritual link which unites in one sole family of adorers the members of the Society of Priest Adorers and those of the Monthly Adoration in the parishes, together with the religious of the Congregation of the Most Holy Sacrament, allows them to be addressed with the same instructions which Père Eymard gave to his sons in his rule, and which are the most perfect expression of his thought and mind. It is, in fact, the same sap which nourishes the religious trunk and the secular branches of the eucharistic tree planted by the venerable founder in order to produce the fruits of love, of honor, of satisfaction, and glory which the divine King of the sacrament desires so greatly and so legitimately to enjoy.

The adoration has a threefold object, and ought to be considered in a threefold relation. It is first Our Lord Jesus Christ that it ought to honor beneath the eucharistic veils; next it is the love of the adorer which it ought to sanctify; and, lastly, it is our neighbor which it ought to assist and to help, and especially the Church.

The Adoration in Relation to Our Lord.

I. That Our Lord Jesus Christ, truly present in the Most Holy Sacrament, has every right to be adored is what His divinity with all His infinite perfections proclaim—His title of First Principle and of Creator of all things; His title of Universal Preserver of all that is; His title of Supreme End and of Sovereign Remunerator.

This is likewise proclaimed by His humanity, deified in the womb of Mary, through personal union with the Word, and then by a fresh title, His glorified humanity at the right hand of the Father in heaven, where, in compensation for His abasement and His death, it received as recompense the exercising of a universal empire.

It is proclaimed not less evidently by the Eucharist—that is to say, the real presence of Jesus Christ under the sacramental veils, through its reality, its perpetuity, and its universality. For if He be present here below, in the verity of His divine and human nature, He claims the adoration due to His divinity and His humanity; if He remains in a constant and assiduous manner which defies time, it is to receive thenceforth, upon earth even as He receives in heaven, the adoration to which He has, since His victory, acquired a rigorous and inalienable right; if He everywhere extends His august and beneficial presence, it is because the empire He has conquered extends over the whole earth, and because He wishes that all nations should recognize it as a fact in all places.

This, then, is the fundamental reason, and which is obligatory on all men, of the adoration—namely, to render to Jesus Christ—God, Man, and King—present in the sacrament, and just on account of that very presence, all the adoration due to Him by these titles.

II. There is still another reason, special to those who have been called in a greater or less measure to the eucharistic vocation. For twenty years Our Lord spoke to the heart of Père Eymard what the sweet voice of Mary then put in these words: "All the mysteries of my Son have a religious society to honor them; it is only the Eucharist which has none; it must have one!" And Père Eymard, in order to respond to the appeal, founded the Society of the Most Holy Sacrament, consecrated to the sole service of the Eucharist, of which the essential act is the perpetual and solemn adoration of this august sacrament.

The sacramental Christ specifies therefore for us His rights and His will to be adored in the Eucharist; He makes of it a personal obligation, the most important duty of our individual vocation. It is evidently tantamount to desiring us to consider the adoration as our supreme object here below, our one sole business, the goal of all our efforts.

He seems to say to us: "Every one owes Me faithful and assiduous adoration in My sacrament; many absolutely refuse it to Me;

"A great number of those who render Me this homage do not do so sufficiently or generously enough;

"No one makes this adoration his supreme duty, his sole occupation, his life. And yet *unum est necessarium*, one sole thing is absolutely necessary, before and above all others: it is that God and I, Jesus Christ, the Son of His complaisance, should be adored!

"Let you, at least, give Me this homage, give Me the satisfaction of rendering the adoration which is due to Me, to My Father and Me, which I came to seek in making Myself man, and which I pursue in remaining in the Eucharist. Make this adoration your state, your only all!"

Such is the meaning of the Society of the Most Holy Sacrament, and of the individual vocation of all those who are called by divine grace to it.

"The supreme reason of the Society of the Holy Sacrament," says Père Eymard, "consists wholly in this: to give to Our Lord Jesus Christ, really present and always remaining in the sacrament for love of men, true and perpetual adorers and propagators of His eucharistic glory, that Jesus Christ may be adored in communities throughout the whole world. Also, let all who are called be certain that they have given themselves only for one sole object—namely, the service of the adorable person of Jesus Christ in the Eucharist, and that they must consecrate to this service their talents and their gifts, their graces and their virtues, their persons and all that they possess, without keeping anything for themselves, not even their personality: *Absque sui proprio!*"

III. From the foregoing flow two important consequences: First, to appreciate the adoration at its proper value; second, the manner of practising this adoration.

The first consequence: The value of the adoration.

It is a holy service, an angelic function, something wholly divine, since it gives us the reality of our God in His terrestrial presence as the immediate object to honor, to serve, to adore, face to face.

It is a royal service, since it asks us to serve Him on the throne which He assumes here below in order to exercise the functions of His royalty over the world, and to receive its homage in compensation for the humiliations He underwent during His Passion, and of those to which He is being subjected in His eucharistic state.

It is, then, the duty, the task, the most noble, the most elevated, the most glorious of all employments to which life can be devoted, seeing that to satisfy the person and the personal rights of Jesus Christ is evidently superior to satisfying the rights and the needs of our neighbor, who is only a creature : *Optimam partem.*

It therefore possesses the legitimate and well-founded right—absolutely and by itself—of taking the precedence of every other kind of labor, of every other kind of service, and, in case of any competition arising, it requires that everything else should come after and be sacrificed to it. He who acts thus is simply logical in his faith and in his conformity to what is true : *Quæ non auferetur ab ea.* He only renders to the superadorable person of Jesus Christ that to which he has a right. And he who does not render it is either very ignorant or very illogical in his faith, or, lastly, cowardly in presence of the first of all his duties. He disowns in fact, if not formally, Our Lord Jesus Christ, since he places the service of His person in a secondary rank.

Second consequence : The practical spirit of the adoration in regard to Our Lord. Having Our Lord Jesus Christ as an immediate object to be recognized and honored, it requires of us purity and holiness of life. We do not present ourselves in a negligent costume to serve a king upon his throne. In heaven the angels who surround the throne of glory are purity itself, and saints are not admitted to the eternal adoration unless they are purified from the slightest stains not only of sin, but of everything which has the least connection with sin. Is it not the same God of holiness whom we come to adore beneath the veils of the Most Holy Sacrament?

There is needed an immediate or proximate preparation of the mind, of the memory, of the heart; for God is a spirit, and He searches not for those who are merely adorers in nothing more than the outward form, but for adorers who worship Him in spirit and in truth, by means of the whole interior homage of their faculties— faith, love, praise, submission, humility, and interior acts of all the virtues. Now, without a preparation which makes the mind come forth from its habitual occupations and fixes the attention upon a precise point, our soul, absorbed by the immediate cares of sensible things, weighed down beneath the burden of the flesh, is incapable of rising to the region of faith and of giving itself up there to spiritual intercourse with God.

Lastly, we ought to propose to ourselves as the principal object in the adoration to honor, to satisfy, to serve Jesus Christ, infinitely more than the sanctifying of ourselves and the serving of even our spiritual interests. Without excluding this last end, but, on the contrary, favoring it, as we shall see later on, the adoration ought, before all things and above all things, to pursue the first object. It is in its nature : it is the expression of perfect charity, of pure love, which finds its perfection and its repose in the satisfaction of the beloved object, and not in its own satisfaction. Moreover, it is commanded by the immediate presence and the superior rights of Jesus Christ. Is it not the first of all things that God is God and recognized as such? His glory takes precedence of our interests, and we ought to wish it, and to ask for it beyond things which are necessary to us, even if they contribute to this very glory. Is it not thus that the Saviour has taught us to pray in the Our Father, where, before all else, before "our daily bread, our forgiveness, and our preservation from temptation and from evil," He makes us ask for "the sanctification of the name of God, the coming of His reign, the accomplishment of His will"?

Therefore, before all things else, in the first and longest portion of the adoration, we ought to apply ourselves to the recognizing of Our Lord Jesus Christ in His perfections and His mysteries, in His person and in His life, in His words and in His virtues, in all His beauty, His kindnesses, His amiability; above all, in His love, and in His love present in the sacrament, in His tenderness, His bounty, His sacrifice.

We ought to study all these marvels of beauty, grandeur, and truth; we ought to strive to see, to understand, to penetrate by means of a sedulous and active, humble and persevering faith—such is the homage and the gift of the spirit. Having entered into this spirit of faith, our duty now is to love all these amiabilities, to adhere to them, to desire them, to take pleasure in them, and then to praise, bless, and exalt, congratulate, rejoice in our hearts; afterwards to contemplate, to adore, in the silence of amazement, of ravishment, of ecstasy, the last expression of love—such is the homage and gift of the heart. Lastly, to give ourselves, to submit and to conform ourselves to what seems to us to be so beautiful and so good, even as we give ourselves to the Infinite Good, without reserve, without keeping aught back, in order to be possessed, to be dependent, to be vivified, to be assimilated, to be transformed interiorly into the resemblance of the divine object which we adore, that it may be everything within us—authority, principle, and life, and that we may disappear and be lost wholly in it.

Such is the first end to be attained in the adoration, the principal employment of the time consecrated to the adoration—it is the homage of the whole interior being to Jesus Christ, for no other reason than because He supremely merits it; without any other object than that of rendering satisfaction to Him, of honoring Him, of loving Him. In heaven nothing else is done except the loved duty of serving Him, loving and praising Him, giving and losing one's self in God—it is the supreme homage, the most lofty glorification which God can receive from His creatures. The God of the sacrament claims it and expects it. He is there for that purpose; He desires to receive it upon earth, in the manner in which it can be received here below, where faith replaces vision, militant charity consummate love, hope possession, but where faith, hope, and charity unite us really to Him in the Sacrament of His Real Presence —*Adveniat regnum tuum . . . sicut in cœlo et in terra!*

The Adoration in Relation to Ourselves.

In relation to ourselves the adoration is clothed with a double character : (*a*) It is our principal duty ; (*b*) it is our principal means of sanctification, and this double title lays upon us obligations with which it is necessary to be well acquainted.

I. *Principal duty.* Père Eymard formally declares that "adoration is the supreme object of his institute," and he desires that if it should form apostles "their sole object should be to have the Blessed Sacrament adored by all men throughout the whole world." The fundamental reason of all the secular works which are taken in hand by the Society of the Blessed Sacrament is therefore the adoration. To all, consequently, in the measure in which they are engaged in them, are addressed these other words of Père Eymard, setting forth the great duty of the adoration: " As the service of adoration is of itself the first of all our duties, and ought to be preferred to all the others, let no one omit or postpone or lessen the hours of adoration assigned to him." He also says with incomparable sweetness: " Look, then, at the hour of adoration assigned to you as an hour of paradise; betake yourself to it as if you were going to heaven, to the divine banquet; and then it will be an hour desired and welcomed with rejoicing; keep the desire for it sweetly enshrined in your heart. If you should have an hour which is painful to nature, rejoice all the more, your love will be greater because it will suffer more. If because of an infirmity, illness, or impossibility you should not be able to make your adoration, let your heart be sad for a moment only; then make your adoration in spirit, unite yourself with those who are adoring at that time, keeping yourself during the whole hour in a state of the greatest recollection."

These words clearly intimate that adoration is the first of all our duties, whence it follows that we must attach more importance to it than to anything else whatever, and that if it be not performed, or not performed well enough, loss and injury will be the result.

Thence the necessity of practically recognizing the importance of the adoration by the following means: (*a*) By making it take precedence of study, of the service due to our neighbor, the ministry of souls, preaching, and zeal; of all exercises of private devotion, even of health and the preservation of life; (*b*) by treating it with all the care, with all the attention that it claims—

care in preparing the mind by fixing the subject of the adoration ; care in preparing the heart for it by habitual recollection in the love of Our Lord, *Manete in me, in dilectione mea ;* care in preparing the will, by fidelity to duty, fervor in spiritual work, conformity to the will of God, and abandonment to His good pleasure ; care in preparing the conscience, by means of the purity and the delicacy assured to it by frequent examinations ; care in preparing the body also, by keeping from all excess, even of labor and of zeal, which renders it untidy, through over-excitement or fatigue, to co-operate in the adoration by the recollection of the senses ; lastly, if the adoration is the first duty, everything ought to tend to it and to prepare for it—study and prayer, the holy office, Mass and communion, actions and virtues, labor and mortification, joys and sorrows—the whole life ought to move on this axis and converge towards this centre.

II. *Principal means of sanctification.* The adoration would be imperfect if, tending to honor God, it did not procure the sanctification of the soul. Therefore it is in its nature theoretical and practical, speculative and moral.

It aims at the honor of God in the faith, the love, the praise of the mind, of the heart, and of the will. But God has a right to more than this, and it is the whole life—life in practice, which ought to praise Him by the concert of all the virtues in action. The perfect praise of God is the resemblance to Him in holiness ; it inaugurates itself in a conviction, a desire, a resolution ; it ought to be completed in works. Thus the adoration has a double object : to honor God by means of the interior faculties, then to sanctify man in order that he may give to God the praise of virtues and of good works. But virtues, in order to take root in the soul, have need of the preparatory employment of prayer. It is there, in silence and in recollection, that the supernatural germs open, send forth their first roots, and form their stem, which will very quickly show itself in actions. Prayer is the interior elaboration of holiness. The masters of the spiritual life are at one in teaching that it is an indispensable means of sanctification, especially for the priest and the religious, because it is the sole efficacious means of arriving at the knowledge and the reform of ourselves.

Now, the prayer common to us all is the adoration. We have no other. And could there be any better one than that which takes place at the feet of Jesus, the object, the Master, the means, and the pattern of all prayer which is performed under His eye, in union with His prayer, in the place sanctified for prayer, and where is breathed an atmosphere all impregnated with the graces of prayer? Therefore the adoration ought to produce in us, as does all assiduous prayer, effective sanctification and practical virtues; but it is on condition that we make of it an exercise of knowledge of ourselves and of consequent amendment.

1. In the adoration we strive to attain a knowledge of ourselves, which means (*a*) that we will consecrate a portion of the time of the adoration to a wholly personal labor of examination into our spiritual state, of the discussion of our actions, and of the application to our own life of the practical and moral consequences of our subject of adoration; (*b*) that we should take care to consider in all truths, even the most speculative, the moral teachings which they contain, to choose from time to time, as the subject of our adorations, exclusively positive and practical truths, and, lastly, to choose, in as far as it is possible, such as have relation to the actual state of our souls, the duties of our state, of which the accom-

plishment is urgent, our immediate needs, our present temptations, our ordinary weaknesses.

2. We will occupy ourselves during the adoration with the reform of our morals, the correction of our defects, of our passions, and of our vices; by attentive, precise, and prolonged examinations, discussing everything as to its cause and its effect; by regret, contrition, detestation of the evil which we recognize in ourselves; by formal and precise resolutions having as their object occasions clearly defined.

3. We will apply ourselves therein to the interior exercise of virtues. Every virtue ought first to be practised in the interior kingdom of the intelligence, of the heart, and of the will, from which the King Jesus expects acts so numerous and so precious. The soul ought to be primarily sanctified in its powers in order that afterwards vigorous and frequent exterior acts of the virtues may spring forth. It is our duty to render our faculties exceedingly active by means of the regular and sustained exercise of the virtues suitable to them: to the mind acts of all the intellectual virtues, to the will acts of the moral virtues, to the heart innumerable fruits of love.

There must, therefore, be laid down in the adoration positive and precise acts of the virtues to be encountered in the subject under meditation. For example, in a mystery of Jesus to see the humility, the gentleness, the patience which is rendered visible in it, and then not at once to form in the will acts of these virtues is to make an adoration which is incomplete and mutilated.

These acts ought to be as precise, as multiplied, as prolonged as possible; it would be impossible to give them too much intensity; it is the force accumulated in the interior to act afterwards in the exterior life; the development of the latter will be in proportion to the force obtained within.

In order to link together the practice of virtues which ought to be manifested in our life, particularly in the accomplishment of duties belonging to our state of life, with this interior exercise of virtues in adoration, it is necessary to consider the circumstances in which we may find ourselves, the duties which impose themselves upon us, and then to take very clear and very firm resolutions to conduct ourselves in such or such a manner, to avoid such or such an extreme, to make such or such a kind of effort.

As to the time to be employed in this practical employment of sanctification, it may be said that it ought to fill about half the adoration, since, in accordance with the method of the four ends of the sacrifice, the second portion of the hour of adoration is consecrated to reparation and prayer. The reparation quite naturally demands the examination, the discussion of acts, satisfaction by means of regret and change of life. Prayer will not be rightly accomplished unless we ask for definite graces, conformable to the known needs of our souls, with the firm resolution to profit by them—that is to say, to correspond effectively with them. This supposes that we have recognized our needs, and that we have taken the resolution to act with firmness and constancy.

Last counsel. In order to fully accomplish this law of laboring for our personal sanctification in the adoration and deriving all possible fruit from it, it is necessary to keep and continue the same subjects of adoration, on the reform of defects or on progress in virtue, as long as amendment is not recognized or profit obtained. Sanctification is the labor of our life, and each one of the obstacles to be put aside or of the steps to be taken requires long and persevering efforts. But patience obtains everything. To fly from subject to subject is curiosity and frivolity. The labor to acquire holiness is of a very different character. It is regular and serious.

III. Such are the practical rules of the adoration considered in relation to ourselves. If they are neglected the adoration necessarily falls into one of the following defects : (*a*) Pure speculation, study, the exclusive labor of the mind, intellectual curiosity, all which things, put in the place of prayer, are the most substantial of the aliments of spiritual pride ; they lead sooner or later to the strange and fatal alliance of beautiful thoughts, of beautiful imaginary representations on all the truths of religion, and of a life wanting in energy, relaxed, ill-regulated, and finally culpable ; (*b*) an exaggerated sentimentality and the over-excitement of the imagination, which engender an effeminate, egotistical, personal, variable, and inconstant kind of piety, devoid of virtue, without any elasticity, without any strength for making sacrifices ; wherein life is spent in more or less fascinating dreams, in more or less fine projects, in promises lacking in fidelity, in impulses which have no aim, in constant beginnings which are void of any sequel ; and (*c*), lastly, worse still ! spiritual idleness, a kind of somnolence of the mind, of the heart, and of the will, which engenders torpor, then routine, and ends by rendering the adoration absolutely null and void—null as a homage to religion, null as a cause of sanctification.

Hence to weariness in the adoration, to being disgusted with this holy exercise, to infidelity towards this capital duty, there is but a step. But if this last step be taken, it is infidelity to the divine King Himself, it is infidelity to our divine vocation, it is apostasy to the service of the Eucharist !

The Adoration in Relation to our Neighbor.

I. The adoration is too essential a fruit of perfect charity for it not, after having attained its first and adorable object, which is the God-Man of the sacrament, necessarily to bend, by the same movement of charity, to the service of our neighbor. After having attained its first and adorable object—the God-Man of the sacrament—adoration is so essentially a fruit of perfect charity, that it necessarily tends by its own accord to the service of our neighbor. Love of our neighbor is inseparable from the love of God; the first is not only the sign of the second, but its necessary effect, its natural fruit. The same sap nourishes both; they are the two branches of one sole trunk. They grow, blossom, bring forth the same fruits at the same time; but withering and sterility also attack them at the same time and in the same degree. "He who says he loves God and does not love his brother is a liar," said the apostle of charity. The exterior forms of charity towards our neighbor vary, and sometimes reveal themselves only in a very restricted number of acts. That depends upon particular vocations, of which some apply in greater measure to our neighbor and others less. But in regard to love in its basis, to charity, to devotedness of the heart and inmost zeal, no vocation is without it; it is a species of love which ought to be devoid of measure and to keep side by side with the love of God.

In the vocation of the adoration direct acts of ministering towards our neighbor are, as a rule, very limited. They can only occupy a portion of our time and of our resources; the first and the greatest belongs to the adoration, to the personal service of the divine King in prayer, to divine praises, and to solemn worship. But that does not dispense us from serving our neighbor with immense love. And it is in the adoration itself that this love ought to be at the service of and procure utility to our neighbor, by means of the apostolate of prayer, propitiation, and reparation.

It is a duty of the vocation. The Society of the Most Blessed Sacrament was founded for the object of apostolic prayer, of reparation for others, of propitiation for the whole world. And could it be otherwise when it requires from its members to remain as suppliants before the throne of grace, where it exposes and causes solemnly to ascend between heaven and earth Him who, says Saint John, "is the Advocate, the just Jesus, the propitiation for our sins, and not only for our sins, but for the sins of the whole world"?

Now, among all our neighbors who have a right to our charity, to our prayers, the first, the most august, that which lays an obligation upon us more strict than any of the others, is the Holy Catholic Church, the spouse so greatly beloved of Jesus Christ, for the love of whom He shed the whole of His blood that "she might become for Him a beautiful spouse, pure, without spot or wrinkle," and for whom He instituted the Eucharist in order to be always present to her, to lead her, to keep her, to defend her, and to nourish her with His substance. To the Church, then, first of all, and to the Supreme Pontiff, in whom she is summed up, must be given the whole of our love, the whole of our devotedness, the whole of our zeal in adoration, in prayer; then to all her members, in the order in which they are placed by their participation of her authority, her holiness, and her life; to bishops, to priests, and to apostolic laborers; to the faithful, to sinners, to those even who reject her in spite of her having over them all the rights of her royal Spouse, to whom "has been given all nations to be His inheritance ;" to heretics, to schismatics, to Jews, and to infidels.

And beyond this world, in the dark prisons of purgatory, our charity ought to be exercised, in the person, so interesting, so worthy of pity and love, of the suffering Church.

It is hardly necessary to say that all the special obligations which may impose a tribute of charity on a person, through the ties of blood or of supernatural affinity or of gratitude, ought to be respected and satisfied in the apostolical ministry of the adoration. And among these ties, which are created by grace, none is more sacred or stronger than that which links souls together in the unity of a religious family or in an association recommended by the Church. To our brethren, therefore, members of the same eucharistic body, and to the society which keeps us together, and which bestows on us all the graces of our holy vocation, should be given an excellent part in the devotedness of our filial and grateful charity.

But let the Father say to us, with the authority of a founder, what the adoration ought to be for us in regard to our neighbor :

II. " The adorer should devote himself to the sublime ministry of the adoration as the deputy of the society and of the Church."

Prayer is one of the essential ends of the adoration, according to the method of the *four ends of the sacrifice;* it ought, therefore, to occupy a normal time, the quarter of the adoration.

"Supplication or impetration," says the Father, "ought to crown your adoration and be the glorious trophy of it. Impetration is the strength and the power of eucharistic prayer. Every one cannot preach Jesus in the pulpit, nor labor directly for the conversion of sinners and the sanctification of souls. But all adorers have the mission of Mary at the feet of Jesus—that is, the apostolical mission of prayer, of the eucharistic prayer, in the midst of the splendors of worship, at the foot of the throne of grace and of mercy. The eucharistic prayer goes direct to the heart of God like a burning dart; it makes Jesus labor, work, and live again in His sacrament; it lets loose His power. The adorer does still more than this; he prays through Jesus Christ; he places Him on His throne of intercession near the Father, as the divine advocate of His redeemed brethren.

"Your mission is to ask grace with Him for all the guilty, to pay their ransom to the divine mercy which has need of suppliant hearts; it is to make you victims of propitiation together with Jesus the Saviour, who, not being able to suffer any longer in His risen state, will suffer in you and by you.

"These words, *Adveniat regnum tuum!* ought to be the motto, as it were, of the prayer of the adorers. Let them offer their adorations for the Supreme Pontiff and for all his intentions, for the exaltation of our holy mother, the Church, for the obtaining of the blessings of God upon the society and the sanctification of their brethren; for all persons occupying offices of dignity, as well in the Church and religion as in the State; especially for all priests in order that Jesus may live in them by love and holiness; for the destruction of heresies and schisms, for obtaining the recognition of Jesus Christ by the Jews, the adoration of the Saviour by pagans; lastly, for the whole world, that all men may love Our Lord Jesus Christ, and may hasten to His sacrament of life."

III. It follows from these words and from the considerations which precede them, that we have in the adoration a real ministry of charity to accomplish towards our neighbor. In it we ought to be propitiators, advocates, mediators, apostles.

To think in it only of ourselves, to pray in it only for our personal interests, however holy they may be, is, therefore, not enough ; we' ought to form for ourselves in it generous, disinterested, devoted hearts open to all the interests of Jesus Christ ; to the needs of the whole world. The great desires, the consuming ardors, the holy tortures of anguish for souls and for the Church ought to inflame and consume our hearts.

It will suffice for this purpose to remember how extensive, immense, and infinite is the work of this redemption of the world which the divine Saviour pursues in His prayer and in His perpetual immolations in the sacrament. He labors therein day and night ; and what labor ! what ungrateful labor, thwarted, combatted, coming into constant collision with obstinate malice, with base treachery, with deep, unceasing hatred ! It is to such a task as this that He invites us. And as it is in prayer and secret immolation He first pursues it, it is the ardor and the assiduity of our supplications, of our cries and of our tears, that He desires from us ; it is the sacrifice of all secret pains, of all the tortures of the soul, of all the mortifications known to Himself alone, that He expects from us.

Ah ! who would refuse Him this hearty and joyful acceptance of humiliations, of being subjected to contempt, treachery, and abandonment, of calumny, accusations, and unjust condemnations ; who would refuse Him the privation of all joy in prayer, in the spiritual life of all consolation, in labor of all personal success, in our whole life of all satisfaction, in order to complete His Passion, and to co-operate by these means in obtaining His eucharistic reign, or the exaltation of the Church, or the deliverance of the Supreme Pontiff, or the conquest of an infidel country ; or the consolidation and the prosperity of the society devoted to the sole service and the sole apostolate of His sacrament of love ; or the success of some special work, known to every one, and to which they are attached by personal ties of vocation or of predilection—the conversion of a parish, the conversion or sanctification of a single soul, especially if it be the soul of a father, of a husband, or of a son, still more, if it be a soul from which God seemed, by the exquisite gifts He had lavished upon it, to expect more of satisfaction, more of glory !

Such is the adoration with regard to our neighbor : a work of perfect charity, of apostolic zeal, of universal and indefatigable devotedness. Its means are chiefly prayer and interior immolation. But it must be remembered that the condition which is indispensable to every mediator, desirous of being listened to, is purity, holiness, separation from sin, and a supernatural life ; it is, at any rate, by these features that Saint Paul represents to us the Eternal Pontiff and the Perfect Adorer, Our Lord Jesus Christ ; it is at this price alone that our prayer, united with His, will be agreeable to God : *Talis enim decebat ut nobis esset pontifex, sanctus, innocens, impollutus, segregatus a peccatoribus et excelsior cœlis factus.*

II. The Method of Adoration by Means of the Four Ends of the Sacrifice.

The Idea of the Method of the so-called Four Ends.

Every art, in addition to its general principles, has its method—that is to say, an elementary discipline, a certain manner of procedure—by means of which disciples are initiated into the knowledge of the art, and then into its easy practice, finally into its secrets and its perfection. Illustrious masters, saints, have given different methods of the great art of prayer, the excellence of which does not stand in any need of demonstration. They have characteristics common to them all, having all of them a double, necessary object—namely, that enabling the soul to glorify God by means of the homage of an interior religion, and next to sanctify itself through the contemplation of the eternal truths, the knowledge of itself, and the preparation of its duties. They vary according to the special point of view which their authors have placed before them and the special object which they desire to attain.

When prayer has for its special end the fashioning of the servant of God for the performance of good works, or for arming the soldier of Christ for holy combats, the method demands much from the labor of the mind through reflection, interior discussions, and study; it aims, above all, at practical results, strong and precise resolutions of the will which lead immediately to action. If, on the contrary, prayer is destined primarily to permit the soul to find God in order to converse with Him and to unite itself with Him in the active repose of love; if it aim at making a contemplator rather than a laborer, an adorer rather than an apostle, the method will demand less of an abstract labor from the mind, less of actual resolutions and of precise determinations from the will. Without neglecting these things, and in giving them a legitimate and necessary part, it will rather look for a simple glance from the mind, for sentiments of the heart, for peaceful acquiescences of the will. It will fix the gaze of the soul upon God, upon Jesus, His mysteries and their spirit, upon His interior and His sentiments, more often than on itself, upon its duties to be accomplished, and its passions to be repressed. Not, once more, that it excludes the labor of sanctification, that necessary homage of all true religion, in the same manner as the method of prayer which forms the apostolical laborer does not exclude union with God, repose in God as at least the term of its different acts. But in the combination of these two essential elements of prayer the one method will give more to labor in regard to self, and the other more to the contemplation of God; the former will be directed more towards the discussion of personal acts, the latter to the praising of the divine perfections.

Father Eymard, when replacing in his plan of spiritual life, such as he established it for souls called to serve the Eucharist, prayer by the adoration of the Most Holy Sacrament, was constrained to adopt a method which should, above all, favor contemplation, praise, conversation, and union with God. The adoration, in fact, must be made before the Most Holy Sacrament, whether at the foot of the throne of the Solemn Exposition or before the tabernacle, the burning lamp of which is a sign of the living Christ who inhabits it.

The mere fact of such a presence claims that the adorer, coming forth from out of himself, should fix all the thoughts of his soul on the august person of the God-Man shown to him through the transparent veils of the sacrament. It would seem as though it would be almost a violation of the highest rules of propriety to be occupied with ourselves rather than with Him, and as though we did not take sufficient account of what His near presence claims from us. However necessary may be the study and the reformation of ourselves, it would seem as though, in presenting Himself so openly before our eyes, the hidden God, who so greatly desires to be known, were soliciting us to study Him, to know Him, to apply ourselves to Him first before descending afterwards into ourselves, assured, as we may well be, that we shall never see as well what we are as after we shall have clearly seen what He is—*Noverim te, noverim me!*

But, more than this, desiring that the adorer should unite his prayer with that which, from behind the eucharistic veil, the real Holy of Holies, Jesus, the one sole Pontiff, offers to His Father, and which is only the continuation of His sacrifice—that is to say, of His death, accomplished in the morning on the altar, Father Eymard was obliged to seek for a method which would permit the adorer to appropriate to himself the acts, the homage, the sentiments, the duties, of which the Mass is the solemn and perfect expression. Now, by the Mass, or by His sacrifice, Jesus Christ renders to God four principal species of homage which the Council of Trent defines: adoration, thanksgiving, reparation or propitiation, and prayer. These four species of homage include all the duties of religion—that is to say, a theoretical and practical recognition of all the truths which attach men to God. Saint Thomas has defined in the following brief and profound words the religion of man towards God: " Man is linked and bound to God, above all, for these four reasons—namely, on account of His supreme majesty, composed of all His divine excellences ; on account of His past benefits, testimonies of His goodness and of His love ; on account of the offences committed against His holiness, which render him a debtor to His justice ; and on account of the possessions which are necessary to him for the future as regards time and eternity, and which he cannot obtain except from His liberal bounty, which is rich in all kinds of possessions."*

---

* Homo maxime obligatur Deo propter majestatem ejus, propter beneficia jam accepta, propter offensam et propter beneficia sperata. 1a 2æ q. CXII., a. III., ad. 10.

Each one of these different species of homage includes the most precious and necessary acts of virtues; they contain all that can be expressed of the recognition of the perfections and of the rights of God; the confession of all the duties, of all the obligations imposed upon man. For, in reality, there is only one prayer which is perfect in all respects—namely, Holy Mass; all other prayers are valuable only in proportion to their more or less great union with this personal prayer of Jesus Christ. It is the same with the Christian virtues, which compose, together with the homage of prayer, the religion of man towards God; the only value they possess is in the measure in which they take their origin and are consummated in the sacrifice of Jesus Christ. For a Christian there is, therefore, no form of prayer more perfect than the participation in spirit and in truth in the holy sacrifice.

But it must be borne in mind that during the time in which Christ preserves the state of an immolated Victim, with which He clothes Himself while offering to His Father His mysterious but real death in the sacrifice of the Mass, the religion which is then expressed, the homage which is then rendered, He continues, by the continuation of the said state, to render to His Father. During the whole of every day and every night, in the permanence of this state of Victim beneath the species of bread and wine, He adores the majesty, thanks the goodness, makes reparation to the justice, implores the liberality of God.

This it is which inspired Father Eymard with his method of adoration, called by him *the method of the four ends of the sacrifice*. Placing the adorers in the presence of Jesus, the perfect Adorer, could he ask of them anything more opportune, more suitable, more necessary even, than to unite himself to the Master of prayer, to the Pontiff in the exercise of his prayer, and to pray like Him, with Him, by Him?

He therefore asks of his disciples to aim primarily, in their adorations, at the production of acts of adoration, of thanksgiving, of reparation, and of prayer; to address them to God the Father, by Jesus Christ, the Mediator and Pontiff; to address them to Jesus Christ Himself, who is God as well as Priest, and the eternal end of all things, at the same time as a Mediator between His Father and men.

But as all these species of homage ought to spring from everything which God has revealed to us respecting His excellences, from all that His bounty has given us, from all that we owe to His justice, from all that we expect from His infinitely bountiful plenitude, Father Eymard teaches his disciples to discover in all truths, all mysteries, in all subjects of meditation, in one word, the motives of adoration, of thanksgiving, of reparation and of prayer which they necessarily contain. He teaches them what acts of virtue are inferred by each one of these species of primordial homage in order to be properly rendered, some virtues being more suitable to adoration, others to thanksgiving, others to reparation, and others, lastly, to prayer. Finally, these motives not being able to be discovered, and these acts to be produced, except by a certain labor of the faculties and of the powers, Father Eymard demands from the intelligence, the heart, and the will their regular co-operation, which is what all the different methods of prayer claim. In this manner the whole of the interior being is seen to be employing itself in successively producing, in union with the Eucharistic Pontiff, the homage of the great and perpetual prayer of this sacrifice.

From the strictly methodical point of view each of these species of homage ought to succeed one another in the order in which the Council of Trent enumerates the ends of the eucharistical sacrifice: Adoration—Thanksgiving—Reparation—Prayer. Father Eymard even recommends that the hour of adoration (for he asks that the adoration should habitually last an hour) should be divided into four quarters, and that each quarter should in turn be consecrated to rendering to God the four great species of homage. He does not, however, render such an equal partition of time absolutely necessary and obligatory, and if grace gives one inspiration any one species of homage may be prolonged beyond the others. But whatever may be the length of time given to each species, the succession of these four thoughts singularly facilitates the exercise of the adoration, even in the case of the most inexperienced. It is then four successive prayers, each of a quarter hour's duration, linked together by the unity of the same subject, but varying by means of the four different points of view under which they are made to pass; and each time all the faculties are brought into play in order to derive from them the diverse motives of the four ends and to produce the acts of virtue proper to each. What could be simpler or easier? The same truth, taken up again and replaced four times under a different aspect: (1) Of the adoration or of the divine excellences reflected in it; (2) of the thanksgiving, and of the features of the divine goodness which it bears, and the benefits it recalls to mind; (3) of the reparation, and of the differences it manifests between what we are and what we ought to be in order to accomplish the duties it reveals to us; (4) of prayer and of the graces which we need in order to fulfil the obligations it imposes on us.

Such is the method of the four ends of the sacrifice. Can we not see that by means of this method of adoration our prayer is made to participate in a wholly special manner in the august prayer of Jesus Christ, and that we unite our own private religion to the public religion of the holy sacrifice? that we are consequently placed in very near relations with the Eucharistic Pontiff, and that we honor in a very direct manner His state and His action in the sacrament? What could be more appropriate to a prayer which is destined to be offered in the presence of the tabernacle, or of the throne of the exposition?

To facilitate the exercise of it we now proceed to enumerate the acts of the different virtues which may be produced by our different faculties for the purpose of expressing the homage of each one of the four ends of the sacrifice. Certainly we are not bound each time to make acts of all these virtues; we name them all in order that a person may choose among them according as the nature of the subject or the state of his soul and the movement of grace may guide him.

III. Acts of the Faculties and of the Virtues in Each of the Four Ends.

Acts and Virtues of the First End.

Adoration, understood as the first of the ends of the sacrifice, has as its object the recognition of the divine majesty, says Saint Thomas, *propter majestatem*, and, as he says elsewhere, that which evidences His excellence above His creatures, the beauty, the perfection, the amiability of God—all that constitutes His infinite being. In relation to us, it is His sovereign rights as First Principle and Supreme End, of Creator and Preserver.

The acts of the mind, in the adoration, are faith in the truth proposed as the subject of adoration, because of the divine word and authority; the supernatural *understanding* of the truth in question ; the spiritual *contemplation* of the perfection and the amiability of God which are manifested therein ; *admiration ; praise*.

The acts of the heart, or of the affective will, are *complaisance, desire, good-will, joy*.

The acts of the will, properly so called, are *the gift, the giving up, of ourselves* to the excellences, the perfections, the amiabilities, the rights, the sovereignty of God ; and this gift can hardly be manifested except by a kind of *annihilation of ourselves* in the presence of so much greatness, of so much splendor, of rights so lofty, of a majesty so sublime. *Humility, absolute submission, abandonment without reserve, holy fear, religious and profound silence*, are the expressions most suitable for rendering this annihilation of the creature in presence of his Creator whom he adores.

Acts and Virtues of the Second End.

The action of thanksgiving has for its object the gifts, the benefits of God : *propter data*, such as they are manifested in the truth which we are meditating ; consequently its formal object is the goodness and the love of God, proved by His benefits.

The acts of the mind are the following : *Consideration* of the portion exercised by the goodness, the love of God in the proposed truth, by means of the views and the merciful designs revealed in it ; *remembrance and enumeration* of the benefits relating to this truth which we have received in our past life, or which we are still receiving every day ; the *study* of the value, of the greatness, of the magnificence of these benefits, drawn from the different circumstances which render them more or less costly ; the *gratuity of them, the greatness of the donor, the indigence and the unworthiness of the* recipient, *the continuation of the gifts,* in spite of abuse or of the small profit derived from them, *admiration, praise.*

The acts of the heart are *grateful love, complaisance and joy, benediction and jubilation, effusions of gratitude and of tenderness, happiness and repose, the silence of beatitude.* These acts issue from the considerations exercised by the mind as enunciated above, the heart following upon the mind at the sight of the divine goodness and the review of His gifts.

The acts of the will are *effective gratitude, testified by protestations of fidelity,* towards a benefactor so magnificent; *humility* or the very humble acceptance of the position of *debtor* and of an *insolvent debtor; resolutions to make use of all of His gifts only for His glory,* to render to Him the fruit of these seeds of His liberality; *promises* to make returns to Him for them; lastly, the gift of ourselves, of all that we have, of all that we are, of all that we will do, *in testimony of gratitude and as an instalment of our debt.*

Acts and Virtues of the Third End.

Propitiation or reparation has for its object the offences and the shortcomings to be found in our life in relation to the truth which we are meditating, and which this meditation discovers to us: *propter offensam.* Reparation first supposes the confession of the fault committed against the holiness of God and the acceptance of the debts contracted towards His justice; then, by prayer, the re-entering into favor through His mercy. The formal object of reparation is, therefore, justice to be appeased and holiness to be restored, then the mercy of God to be gained.

Acts of the mind: *The examination, or the attentive consideration* of the contrast between our life and the truth proposed to it, either through our formal sins or through our imperfections; *meditation upon the seriousness of the state in question,* upon the *gravity and the number of our faults; upon the consequences* which such a state and such faults bring with them in regard to God, to Jesus above all ; in regard to our responsibilities towards our neighbor ; in regard to our vocation in time and our eternal future ; and the sincere and humble *confession* of all our sins.

Acts of the heart : They consist chiefly in *saddened love, compunction, a breaking of the heart, contrition;* regret, bitterness, salutary fear, holy sorrow, horror of sin ; *compassion, pity for ourselves and the other victims of sin—compassion, above all, for Jesus,* the first, the universal, but the innocent. the gentle victim of our sins.

Acts of the will : *Detestation and renunciation of evil, shunning the occasions leading to it, the rupture of its ties, interior conversion, a firm resolve; satisfaction and the resolution to perform penance; voluntary humiliation*, the acceptance of all the pains it may please God to inflict upon us in expiation of our faults ; lastly, the *gift of ourselves,* in the humble annihilation of the sinner, to justice that it may satisfy itself here below in regard to us ; to mercy that it may have pity on us, have patience and give us new graces ; to holiness that it may restore and transform us.

Acts and Virtues of the Fourth End.

Supplication, or prayer, has for its object the gifts, the benefits, and the graces of God to be obtained in the future even as the act of thanksgiving had for its object the giving thanks for benefits already received : *propter beneficia sperata.* It has as its express reason the goodness, the liberality, the plenitude, the providence of God, which it takes upon itself to touch and to render attentive and generous in giving us all the good things necessary to our indigence as being creatures of nothingness. The view of the indigence in question had already appeared during the *reparation*, in the consideration of the shortcomings and faults which disfigure our souls with respect to the truth proposed as a subject ; it had already appeared in the contrast between these defects and the divine perfections contemplated in the *adoration*, with the benefits and the gifts set forth in the *act of thanksgiving*.

Acts of the mind : A clear view of our needs ; *a consideration* of the exact species of graces we have to seek in order that our soul may profit by all the fruits contained in the proposed truth ; the *consideration* of the *riches*, of the *plenitude*, of the *providence* of God, which possesses, without impoverishing itself, wherewith to enrich millions of creatures who are nothingness ; a *remembrance* of the *promises* whereby God has engaged Himself to give either by way of *facts* or of *guarantees* which show that He will be still more liberal, having already been so in such a magnificent manner.

The acts of the heart consist in *hope, confidence, desires*, which are ardent and lively, animated as they are by the *sentiment* of what we *have already received ;* in the *suffering* we experience because of our indigence ; in *pity* for ourselves and for others whose needs we know to be identical with ours ; in *charity*, disinterested *love* which is *generous, zealous, apostolical*, and makes us desire and earnestly ask what will be either for the glory of God or a benefit for our neighbor.

The acts of the will are *formal prayer* or the *supplication* expressed by the heart or the lips ; *repeated, instant, persevering prayer ; humble, lowly prayer*, full of *ardor* and also at the same time of *abandonment*, *willing* what it asks, but still more the good pleasure of the divine will which may prefer, for reasons known to its unfathomable wisdom, to delay instead of immediately granting ; to permit the accomplishment of the trial instead of preservation from it ; the *resolution to carry out into action*, immediately and very faithfully, the graces which are asked for ; the *demand* of the same gifts for *all those who have need of them* ; lastly, the *gift of ourselves*, the oblation of our being and of the whole of our life to the good God from whom we expect help in order to repay it, at least in a slight proportion, by means of this offering of small value, although it be all that we can offer of what is best.

In terminating, a look must be cast upon the duties which will immediately follow upon the adoration : to ask the exact kind of graces which will then be necessary to us, afterwards to implore through Mary and through Saint Joseph the blessing of Our Lord.

The subjects of adoration which are about to be given are composed solely upon these different acts ; if we have not always specified or placed them in methodical evidence, it is in order to permit the pious adorer to express them himself as he may be inspired to do so. We believe that if it be well to help and to enlighten prayer there must be left to each several soul the task and the consolation of making it.

THE EUCHARISTIC CHRIST.

The Institution of the Eucharist.

THE FACT.

I. ADORATION.

ADORE Our Lord, instituting the Sacrament of the Eucharist in the excess of His infinite love.

Contemplate Him on the last day of His life, at the last hour of His liberty, seated in the midst of His apostles, between Saint Peter and Saint John. He has just been humbling Himself in their presence to the extent of washing their feet; they are struck with astonishment, stupefied; what, then, is about to happen?

Jesus takes the bread, raises His eyes to heaven, gives thanks to His Father, blesses the bread, saying, "Take ye and eat; this is My body which is given for you. Do this for a commemoration of Me."

In like manner He takes the chalice filled with wine mixed with water. He blesses it, gives thanks, and says, "Take ye all of this and drink; this is the new testament in My blood, which shall be shed for many unto the remission of sins."

Adore Jesus in these different acts; listen to His

words; hearken to them attentively with the reverence of love. See what sweet majesty is diffused over the whole of His person, what kindness beams from His eyes; what an accent of tenderness there is in His voice!

Then make a formal and detailed act of faith in the whole of this mystery.

I adore, O Jesus, Thy veracity; I believe that Thou hast really pronounced these adorable words; I believe that they are true, and that they will efficaciously produce that which they enunciate.

I believe, then, that the bread becomes, through Thy word, Thy very body, and the wine Thy very blood.

I believe that the whole substance of the bread and of the wine was changed, transubstantiated into Thy body and into Thy blood.

I believe that there remained of the bread and of the wine nothing more than the appearances, the accidents, such as the color, the taste, the weight, and the figure, and that Thy omnipotence alone sustained these accidents.

I believe that Thou wert as truly present then beneath the consecrated species as Thou wert at the table beneath the eyes of Thy apostles.

I believe that the whole of Thy blood was united with the substance of Thy body under the appearance of bread, and the whole of Thy flesh was united with the substance of the blood under the appearance of the wine.

And I believe, O Jesus, that what Thou didst then at the Last Supper priests now do, like Thee, by Thy order and Thy power, in virtue of those words, "Do this for a commemoration of Me."

I believe that Thou art present in all the consecrated Hosts, in all the tabernacles throughout the world, and I adore Thee therein, I praise Thee therein, I bless Thee therein, O Jesus, the Author of this sacrament of love!

I unite my adoration and my faith with that of the apostles at the Last Supper ; I adore Thee with the angels who watch, silent and burning with love, around Thy tabernacles.

II. THANKSGIVING.

" Jesus gave thanks—*gratias egit.*"

O Jesus, Thou givest thanks that the moment has come in which Thou canst give free course to Thy love and allow it to pass over all imaginable limits.

Thou thankest Thy Father for permitting Thee to give Thyself up to every one of us, forever, without reserving anything for Thyself, either of Thy being, or of Thy glory, or of Thy rights !

Thou art happy because of it ; and Thou dost express Thy gratitude even as though it were a gain, a profit for Thee.

What,.then, dost Thou personally gain in giving Thyself thus ? What dost Thou hope to derive in regard to Thyself from this excess of love? Will praises and homage compensate for the forgetfulness, the contempt, the insults with which Thou wilt be assailed during the long sacramental life which Thou dost begin at this hour?

Wilt Thou receive as much love as Thou wilt receive ingratitude?

Dost Thou believe that such a treasure will be esteemed in accordance with its value?

Ah ! Thou knowest what a bitter chalice, always full, always overflowing, this sacramental state prepares for Thee ; Thou knowest in all its most exact details all that awaits Thee ; Thou dost foresee all the circumstances of human malice, Thou dost count all its repetitions, Thou dost measure the whole of its obstinacy ; nevertheless Thou dost give thanks because Thou wilt do good to many souls, and because to do good to Thy poor creatures is Thy supreme object, Thy joy, Thy recompense, the always longing, never satisfied need of Thy heart!

But if Thou dost render thanks because Thou art able to give Thyself, what ought to be my gratitude for receiving this gift of Thy infinite love?

It is for me, for us, that Thou dost institute this sacrament—*pro nobis*.

For me the thought, the sublime invention of the Eucharist!

For me the marvels of power and the multitude of miracles which its institution required!

For me the efforts of love, of patience, of pardon, and the numberless and inexpressible sacrifices which its perpetuity costs! for me, for my good, my salvation, my strength, my assistance, my consolation!

For me! And what am I? Nothingness and sin, weakness and ingratitude.

And Thou, who givest Thyself thus, what art Thou not? All being, all perfection, all love!

O love, O goodness, O condescension, the inexhaustible treasures of the tendernesses of the heart of Jesus, what shall I render Thee?

At least I can confess my insolvable debts; I avow, I confess to Thy glory, that I owe Thee everything, O Jesus! I thank Thee for all, I bless Thee for all.

And I will praise, I will forever chant the blessed hour of the institution of Thy sacrament and of my sacrament; it is the source which will never dry up, the ever-active principle, the inextinguishable hearth of life, of grace, of mercy in the Church.

It is from it that came to me the Host full of pure delights of my First Communion; it is from that blessed source that I gather every morning the strengthening food that fortifies my feeble life ; it is because the hour of the institution lasts always, fixed like a sun in the firmament of the Church that I hope for the Viaticum of my last hour ; it is from Thee, O Jesus in the Eucharist, that I await my eternal heaven !

It is there, in the days which will have no evening, that I shall render Thee worthy thanks for the institution of Thy sacrament, where my intelligence shall have been enlightened to understand the marvels of it, my heart inflamed with infinite love, so as to love it sufficiently, but even in heaven will my gratitude ever rise to the height of the treasure of Thy Eucharist? . . .

III. Reparation.

When instituting the Eucharist the Lord said : " This is My body, which is given, delivered up for you ; this is My blood, which is shed for many unto remission of sins."

These words show that the Eucharist is a sacrifice, an immolation, a death for sin.

In point of fact, is it not equivalent to death for a living man to be reduced to the state of a host, which makes of him the food of man ? There is no longer any brilliancy in his eyes, any majesty in his person, no longer any life upon his lips ; silence, obscurity, inertia, death ! See if there be any greater distance between a living man and his corpse than between Jesus seated at table with His apostles and Jesus become the bread which they eat in trembling.

The eucharistic state, therefore, is like unto a state of death.

The profound humiliation of Jesus in the Host is necessary in order to be in opposition to our pride ; His obedience, to our continual revolts, and His poverty, to the follies attendant upon our luxury.

Holy Father, receive this Host for my sins! Jesus! I ask of Thee pardon for all my sins and the persistent malice I show in repeating them when Thou dost accept such great sacrifices in order to expiate them! I detest them with Thee, like Thee, as much as Thee!

In addition to this state of death, which Thou didst Thyself choose, at the hour of the institution of the Eucharist, how many deaths full of ignominy do we not impose on Thee, O divine Victim! The death of isolation, the death of insult, the death of ingratitude, the death of sacrilege!

And Thou dost see them displayed before Thee, hideous, threatening, contemptuous, outrageous, in the odious person of Judas! But woe to those who inflict them upon Thee! Pardon them, O Jesus! Pardon all those who forsake Thee, despise Thee, and insult Thee! Accept my faith, my respect, my poor love in reparation!

"This is My blood, which is shed for many unto remission of sins" (Matt. xxvi. 28). What does "many" mean if it be not that this blood given for all will not serve all in reality, and that there will be hardened souls who will obstinately turn aside from its redeeming action?

Alas, we see only too clearly that it is so! The blood may flow without interruption, gush from a thousand sources, that it may everywhere spread its salutary floods, and in spite of it there are souls endued with the fatal facility of escaping from it.

And it is the sight of these poor, erring creatures which made Thee endure, O Jesus, at the hour in which Thou didst institute the Eucharist, the most poignant grief. Thou still seest all of them in Judas; in Judas, who would not allow himself to be touched by any of the marks of Thy tenderness; who communicated in a sacrilegious manner; who died impenitent in spite of the advances, the numberless testimonies of Thy love.

And the sight fills Thee with sadness; it makes Thee shudder; it troubles Thee! In it lies the inexpressible torture of Thy heart, at seeing Thy sacrament remain useless in regard to many souls—this sacrament, which is the proof of so great a love, the fruit of numberless sacrifices, the renewal of Thy death daily resumed and continued.

O Jesus! I compassionate Thy trouble, Thy anguish! I implore Thee in behalf of these hardened souls! I supplicate Thee, above all, to have mercy on the dying who reject, at their last hour, the Viaticum of their eternity!

IV. Prayer.

" Do this in commemoration of Me."

When Jesus has given us all; when, in this sole act of the Supper, He made Himself at once our victim, our nourishment, and our companion—our victim to be immolated down to the very end; our nourishment to be given to all men in all centuries, to the little as well as to the great, to sinners as well as to saints; our companion to guide us, to follow us on every shore, under all latitudes, and to live with us like a father in the midst of his children, and a friend with his friends; when He had made the gift which embraces all plenitudes, and which was none other than that of His divine and human being—gift embracing both time and space —then, in return, He addressed Himself to His apostles, and addressed to us in their person a humble, a touching prayer, " Remember Me!"

Yes! in order to repay Him for a love which is clothed in so many magnificent forms, which is so liberal, so constant, so magnanimous, He asks only a remembrance!

Not to forget that He is there; to remember that He is ever attentive to us; to know that He awaits us and ceaselessly offers us all that He possesses, is all that He wants, all that He requires, all that He solicits from us! He begs us, He conjures us, "Remember Me."

Ah! who could express what love and what tenderness flows from these words of the Saviour! With what sweet and powerful harmony does it not resound in the ear of the heart! Oh, all you poor, infirm, afflicted, tempted, troubled, discouraged, blind, naked, famished sinners, I ask all of you, for your sake and mine, "Remember My Eucharist!"

Saviour of my soul! Jesus in the Eucharist, I will remember Thee! I make at this moment a firm resolution to do so. But Thou knowest what my resolves are worth, what they effect, how long they endure if Thy grace do not anticipate and sustain them.

Do everything, then, Thyself! Grant me this grace and keep it Thyself within my soul, the grace to remember Thee.

Give me grace to think of Thee in Thy sacrament with a constant remembrance, which does not yield either to the preoccupations caused by my daily labor, or to the distractions springing from vanity, or to the temptations of the world, or to the weight of my sorrows.

Give me grace to remember Thy Eucharist everywhere, in the solitude of my home, in my family, in my social relations, everywhere!

May Thy divine remembrance sweeten and sanctify my joys and my pleasures; may it soften, supernaturalize, render profitable and fruitful my sufferings and my tears!

May I remember Thee with loving recollection, with my heart, with a remembrance such as Thou willest it should be, which renders me faithful to Thy sacrament, respectful in its presence, eager to receive it, always worthy of it!

May my whole life be regulated, established for Thee, directed towards Thee, vivified by Thee!

O Eucharist! may Thy remembrance be the sun of my life, the light of my mind, the passion of my heart, the safeguard of my conscience, the purity of my intentions, the moving spring of my conduct, the confident support of my prayer; my faith, my hope, and my love!

May I live only to remember Thee, Sacrament of my Jesus!

THE MASTERPIECE OF GOD.

I. ADORATION.

ADORE the divine power of Jesus displaying the strength of His arm, and accumulating the most astonishing marvels in the institution of the Eucharist. Transubstantiation is its masterpiece, for it contains and sums up all the marvels which He has ever worked in the course of centuries.

With one single word Omnipotence changes bread and wine into the body and blood of Jesus Christ; it is a work of as great a power as that of the creation. For it causes to disappear and, as it were, replunges into nothingness the whole substance of the two elements. Now, in order to make a being return into nothingness requires as much power as to draw it out of nothingness; and even then God has to conquer the natural inclination of His goodness which tends rather to expand being than to restrict it.

Then, again, the accidents or the appearances of the bread and of the wine remain in their original state, with the same taste, the same aspect, the same form, the same weight as before. Therein is another marvel, for these appearances cannot, according to the laws of nature, exist without being borne, and sustained, and without reposing upon the substance for which they are created, as upon their natural basis. The body of Jesus is not their point of support, for it has neither the form, nor the whiteness, nor the taste of the Host. Who, then, sustains in their solitude, and suspended, as it were, over the abyss of nothingness, without falling into it, these fragile beings, which cannot subsist by themselves, and which the body of Jesus does not bear up? Omnipotence!

Jesus is thirty-three years of age when He institutes the Eucharist; He is in the maturity of manhood, of lofty stature, strong and agile of limb, with noble features, such, finally, as the first man who had issued from the hands of the Creator; now, in a moment this man is reduced to a point, preserving neither dimensions, nor shape, nor height, nor quantity; all has disappeared, and the eyes see nothing of Him except the veil of bread which covers Him like a pall; who, then, was able to exercise this astounding power upon the body of Jesus? The arm of Omnipotence!

And in this point of consecrated bread, imperceptible, indivisible, inaccessible to the eyes, to the hand, as well as to the understanding of man, Christ continues to be living, complete, organized, in the perfectly harmonized proportions of His body, with all its members, with His face and its sweet expression, with His heart whose palpitations our love or our coldness hastens or abates. What is, then, the hand which thus plays with the most astonishing and, in appearance, the most contradictory of marvels? The hand of Omnipotence!

And as this adorable kind of recreation is sufficiently

agreeable to love, the Omnipotence which inaugurates it in the Last Supper continues it throughout the ages; it confides the admirable means of performing it to poor ministers, taken from among men, and, behold! at every hour of the day, upon the whole surface of the globe, millions of priests recommence and perpetuate these fathomless prodigies without any effort, by the most simple of actions, through only pronouncing a few words in a whisper!

Who among us thinks of this incessant action of the Almighty which transforms the earth into a field of innumerable marvels? Who thinks of it to adore, to bless Omnipotence and to live in the holy fear with which we ought to be inspired by His presence which envelops us, His action which is exercised so close to us, and these marvels strewed beneath our feet, amid which we pass without taking even the least notice of them, like those Eastern monarchs accustomed to tread upon carpets of cloth-of-gold, each one of which is worth the cost of a province?

Omnipotence of Jesus, I adore Thee! The Eucharist is the greatest of all Thy works; Thou alone couldst create it, Thou alone canst maintain it. I know that when love desires it all is possible to Thee, and I believe in all the marvels that Thou dost amass in the Eucharist!

II. THANKSGIVING.

Thank the divine wisdom for the large share that it takes in the institution of the Eucharist; study the admirable means which it employs, the varied resources which it displays, the prodigies of intelligent tenderness which it accomplishes to adapt the Eucharist to our needs and to make of it the masterpiece of love, of goodness, of sweetness and condescension, which it has known how to render so familiar to us!

We need that our God should make Himself present to us in a manner at once sensible and spiritual, accessible and hidden; sensible, because our soul shut up in the prison of our body can see only through the window of the senses; hidden, because faith exercises itself only through the veils of the incomprehensible; sensible, moreover, that it may help our faith; hidden, that it may temper the splendor of the glorious body of Jesus and lower His majesty.

Wisdom invented the presence under the sensible appearances of bread; we thereby see our God, we know where He is, we go straight to Him without hesitation; and yet we do not see Him; faith has room for its exercise, at the same time that love, encouraged by the discreet veil which covers it, enters into the intimate intercourse of familiar friendship with Him.

We have need to find in a divine and restorative aliment the supernatural life we had lost through eating the forbidden and poisonous fruit. Wisdom placed the very life of God, the life of which it lives itself, in the flesh of Jesus; then it reduced and enveloped it in a particle of bread, that we might receive it without feeling the repugnance which the sight of living flesh would inspire in us, and without the terror and the stupor which Jesus would cause us if He came to us in His natural size.

Lastly, it was necessary that all men, having the same needs, might participate in the same happiness as the apostles at the Last Supper; Wisdom immediately performed the two marvels of the perpetuity and the multiplication of the Eucharist; thanks to these means the Eucharist is reproduced every day in every place and the table is laid everywhere for the food and the consolation of every one.

Eternal wisdom, incarnate wisdom, wisdom which did inspire the harmonies of the Eucharist, how sweet is Thy spirit! To show me Thy tenderness Thou dost give me this heavenly bread which contains all sweetness; Thou didst prepare it expressly for me and didst adapt it so well to its end that it would not be possible for me to imagine anything more accessible to my love, more credible to my faith, nothing which could be more suitable to Thy majesty and more in conformity with my needs! Be blessed, praised, and thanked forever, O Wisdom, eternally loving, eternally amiable, which gives us the Eucharist; Thou art the Eucharist itself, and Thou comest to us in the sweet manna of the sacrament!

III. Reparation.

Contemplate the divine mercy in the part which it took in the institution of the Eucharist. It became a great depository of pardon, expiation, and perpetual reparation for the sins of the world.

Sin continuing, alas! to be committed even after Jesus had died upon the cross to destroy and to expiate it, was it not necessary that the death of Jesus should continue to pursue it and to repair it in proportion to the measure in which it would be committed?

Mercy acted in such a manner as to make the Eucharist not only a sacrament, but a sacrifice; and it placed in that sacrifice the merits, the satisfaction, the efficacies of the sacrifice of the cross. Each day it recommences in our favor its work of Calvary; it immolates Jesus, it consumes the Victim, and it never ceases to keep the world bathed in its redeeming blood.

O mercy, how thou dost cling to forgiveness!

Was it not necessary that each soul should be able to draw near to Calvary, to steep its robe in the blood of the Lamb that it might be purified, drink of this salutary fountain to sanctify itself, and eat its portion of the Victim that it might participate fully in the virtue of the sacrifice of Jesus? Was it not a necessity that sin should be attacked in those deepest retreats of the body and soul of each one of us, where its roots are imbedded, that the most pure flesh should purify our flesh, and that the innocent blood should extinguish the devouring heat of our corrupted blood?

And mercy preserves in the risen flesh of Jesus all the sanctifying virtues of the Victim sacrificed on Calvary; it makes of it a balm, a soothing mixture, a sovereign remedy, and each day it gives it to us in the communion; it enters into us together with the sacred Host, and it applies itself to extinguish, to cut off, to restore, to dress, to bind, to cure; nothing which is wounded, sick, suffering, escapes from its action in the soul and even in the body.

O mercy, how thou dost cling to restore us!

Was it not also necessary that guilty, obstinate men should have above them, praying for them, and averting from their heads the thunderbolts of justice, a Priest who should be holy, innocent, without spot, not standing in need of pardon for himself, and able to offer thenceforth in their favor all His prayers and all His merits, and to enable the voice of His blood, voluntarily shed, to be heard day and night?

And, behold! mercy placed this sovereign Priest, this all-powerful Mediator, this indefatigable Advocate, this vigilant Sentinel in all the tabernacles, in all the Hosts; and it commands them earnestly to plead our cause, to watch continually, to give the alarm, to call for succor, to accept outrages, humiliations, wounds, and even death rather than to desert this advanced guard of protection, this citadel of salvation, which covers the world, defends it, and assures its communications with God. And Jesus remains and accomplishes His mission! And the world lives! And the patience of God is not worn out!

O mercy, how thou dost long not to punish!

What have I to do if it be not to unite myself to Thy designs, to make reparation together with the Victim of the altar; to ask pardon for myself and my brethren, with the Priest of the tabernacle; and to sanctify myself by the daily reception of this host which Thou dost render so salutary, O infinite mercy of my God!

IV. Prayer.

Open your soul; let it be dilated with confidence that it may admire the part taken by the divine liberality in the institution of the Eucharist.

"Lord," the prophet said, "Thou openest Thy hand and fillest with blessing every living creature" (Ps. cxliv. 16). This benediction is the bread blessed and consecrated by Jesus at the Last Supper, by the priest at the altar, it is the Eucharist which the liberality of God sheds upon us with open hands. "Take, eat, drink ye all of this." The liberality of our God, so magnificent in all its works, surpasses all measure here. All, always, every day, everywhere, take and eat, take and drink! It is My body, it is My blood which I give up to you!

But if God gives Himself up to us thus, what will He not give us with Him? Will it be celestial and divine gifts? The Eucharist gives us Divinity itself! Will it be gifts for the soul? It gives us the soul of Jesus!

Health, vigor, and purity of the body? It gives us the body of Jesus! Temporal succor, daily bread, commercial profits, the wages of labor? It gives us all the succor, all the gifts, all the treasures contained in the heart of Jesus!

He who gives what is greatest, can He refuse what is less?

And what the liberality of our God thus bestows on us of gifts, of treasures, of help, of graces, and finally the Eucharist, it gives them to us always, without wearying, to all, without refusing even those who abuse it.

Always, to all! And at what price? At the price of a single desire, of a glance raised to the tabernacle, of a need which is expressed, of misery which is confessed! "Come, come ye all, ye also who have neither gold nor silver, hasten hither in crowds, and buy without spending, without any compensation, buy the bread and the wine which satisfy; come, eat, drink, inebriate yourselves, My beloved!"

Sweet liberality of my God, which longs to heap upon me, to overwhelm me, to crush me beneath Thy benefits, I have confidence in Thee, I address myself without hesitation to Thee, I do not place any limits to my desires. My needs, alas! can hardly have any! Among all the poor whose "eyes are open and raised towards Thee, awaiting all from Thy hand, deign to behold me and to count me and give me, me also, as well as to all the others, my food at the favorable hour!" And this food, O ineffable Liberality, is light, strength, consolation, patience, the love of Thy will and humility; it is the health of the body and of the soul for me and mine; it is all the numberless, incessant succors of which I shall have need to-day and to-morrow, and all the days of my life, till the day when I shall possess

Thee in heaven! Give them to me abundantly, promptly, efficaciously; keep them in reserve for me, and in the hour of my need may they reach me living and conquering, these treasures of Thy Eucharist, where Thou dost reside, and where I shall always find Thee, O Liberality, forever adorable!

THE PRIEST.

I. Adoration.

Unite together all the sentiments of reverence, of veneration, of gratitude, of love, and of faith which are capable of entering into the act of adoration in order to adore Our Lord Jesus Christ as He deserves to be adored under His thrice holy, ineffable, and redoubtable title of Priest! Remove by means of faith the veil of the species, and in the Holy of Holies, where He exercises till the end the supreme function of His eternal priesthood, adore the Supreme Priest—*Tu es sacerdos in æternum.* Thou art Priest, Thou art the Priest, the one, sole, eternal Priest, O Jesus, Son of God made man! Thou art a priest, such as no one has ever been or ever will be; a priest by essence, a priest by nature as well as by election; and Thy election—it is Thine own very nature which has constituted Thee to be the Man-God! Thou art a priest in all the plenitude of the sacerdotal form, in all the perfection of sacerdotal qualities, in all the possible extent of the power, of the action, and of the functions of the priesthood—*Tu es sacerdos!* O Jesus Priest, our Priest, I salute Thee, I praise Thee, I prostrate myself before Thee, I adore Thee, I would, if possible, melt away with gratitude and annihilate myself in reverence before the profound and incomprehensible truth, before the supereminent qualities, before the infinite and ineffable action of Thy name, of Thy perfection, of Thy function of priest—*Tu es sacerdos!*

The primary office of the Christ as mediator is the priesthood, and His first act is to interpose between God and man that He may be the authentic intermediary in their supernatural relations, in their religious connections. *Sacerdos, quasi sacra dans*, says Saint Thomas. The characteristic of the priesthood is to communicate to the people the sacred gifts of God—truth, grace, pardon, supernatural life—and to make the sacred gifts of men—their adorations, their prayers, their offerings—ascend to God. Such is the priesthood ; it is the power given by God to a man, chosen by Him, to offer to Him in the name of mankind the religious homage which it owes Him, in the form in which it will please Him to receive it ; then in return to bring to man the words, the commands, the gifts of God. The priest is, therefore, at once the man of God, His minister towards men, and the man of men, their ambassador, their minister in regard to God. The essential act of the priesthood is sacrifice, the summit of religion whence God bends down towards humanity, united together in its entirety to honor Him by the offering of a victim which expresses all its debts, and where God grants to it pardon, provides it with succor, and assures it of His being supremely satisfied.

Let us concentrate our attention upon the person of our adorable Priest. It is clear that a priest must have a call from God in order to enable him, without sacrilegious temerity, to approach Him and to intercede for his brethren. A delegation of the people would not suffice ; in what manner could it make God enter into an engagement with it? God engages Himself only towards men whom He calls, and these He consecrates—

that is to say, He gives them all the qualities which He desires to find in His priests. When, by what sign, what anointing, and, lastly, by what sacrament, did Jesus consecrate the priest of God and of humanity? Ah! go back to the very source of this life, penetrate into the deepest depth of His being; do you see the moment waited for from the beginning of the world, wherein the Holy Ghost having formed a body of the most pure blood of Mary united it to a soul, the most beautiful of created souls? At that moment, swifter than lightning, but greater than even the moment of the first creation, the Second Person of the Trinity, the Word, unites to Himself this privileged humanity and gives it existence by becoming its own proper person; God, the Father, contemplates His Son, no longer only in His bosom, invisible and spiritual, but as man, made flesh, having His own proper body and a soul; and in spite of this new state, as His word has lost nothing by uniting to Himself this humanity, God the Father says to Him, to this Word, henceforth as truly man by His human nature as He is God by His divine nature : " *Tu es filius meus, ego hodie genui te!* Thou art My Son, O Incarnate Word, I have begotten Thee to-day, as Man-God, even as I have begotten Thee from all eternity, as pure spirit, in My bosom—*Tu es filius meus!*" And at the same time, says Saint Paul, the Father adds, " *Tu es sacerdos in æternum!* Thou art a priest forever!" At one and the same time! It is one and the same thing for Christ to be made the Incarnate Word and the Eternal Priest; the call of God consists in separating this humanity from the mass of human nature, infected by sin, and uniting it to the person of the Word. There, like the flowing of the holy oil poured on the head of the figurative priest, all the perfections, the holiness, the truth, the justice, the life, the beatitude, all the gifts, all the treasures of the Father which belong to the Son by equal right, are diffused in the humanity of the Christ without measure and without reservation. It enjoys all the infinite complaisance of the Father, it receives all the divine gifts, in entering through His person into the possession of the divine nature, the source of all good. It is rendered holy, innocent, spotless, sheltered from all sin, not being in debt in any way towards God. Such is the consecration of our Priest. And at the same time, as He is of all men the entirely perfect, the most noble, the richest of the children of men, and through nature and grace their eldest in every way and by all kinds of titles, He finds in this fact the right of representing them all before God, to sum up in Himself all their homage, all their needs, all their desires, even as the head of a family represents all the members of it. In this, then, consists His priesthood, His double delegation: that of God who consecrates and accepts Him, and that of humanity which delegates and sends Him. O sublime priesthood! Perfect Priest! Superabundant consecration! Jesus, I adore Thee in the plenitude and the perfection of Thy priesthood! Ascend Thy altar, "eternal throne of justice; God, Thy God, He who is Thy Father, has consecrated Thee by the anointing of the most glorious priesthood, above all angels, and above all men, Thy brethren—*Thronus tuus Deus . . . unxit te Deus, Deus tuus, oleo lætitiæ præ consortibus tuis!* It is from Thee that flow, as from their sole created source, all the sacerdotal graces. All those, therefore, who will be called to the exalted honor of the priesthood will participate in Thy incomparable elevation, and ought to show themselves worthy of Thee by means of a holiness which will render them more like to Thee than all their brethren."

II. Thanksgiving.

This sacerdotal consecration of our Priest is as touching as it is sublime. For it is indeed for us, in our name, in order to represent us, that our Elder Brother made Himself a priest. Sinners and guilty, debtors and indigent, we are as powerless as we are unworthy to approach God in order to glorify Him, to appease Him, to solicit anew His benefits. Behold the thrice holy, all-powerful Priest who will always be heard because His infinite merit gives Him a right to be heard—*Exauditus pro suâ reverentiâ*. But His eminent holiness, which places Him so far above the guilty mass, will it not make Him forget or despise the earth? No! divine goodness has wished that on being clothed with all the qualities of a God, He should take all the infirmities, all the miseries, all the weaknesses of man, sin alone excepted. But still more than this, our thrice holy Priest—and, it seems to me, even more merciful than holy—takes the temptation, the responsibility, and the chastisement of sin, of our horrible sins which are our essential evil and the cause of all our innumerable evils. He loads Himself with them that He may know the horror and the misery of them; that He may have always an inexhaustible pity, condescension, mercy, and love for the sinner. Ah! weigh well and enjoy these words which Saint Paul utters in praise of our infinitely good Priest: "Because the children of men are partakers of flesh and blood, He also Himself in like manner hath been partaker of the same, that through death He might destroy him who had the empire of death— that is to say, the devil; And might deliver them, who through the fear of death, were all their lifetime subject to servitude. For nowhere doth He take hold of the angels, but of the seed of Abraham He taketh hold. Wherefore it behooved Him in all things to be made like unto His brethren, that He might become a merciful and faithful high-priest before God, that He might be a propitiation for the sins of the people. For in that, wherein He Himself hath suffered and been tempted, He is able to succor them also that are tempted" (Hebrews ii. 14–18). " Let us go, therefore, with confidence to the throne of grace, that we may obtain mercy, and find grace in seasonable aid. For we have not a high-priest who cannot have compassion on our infirmities, but one tempted in all things, like as we are, without sin" (Hebrews iv. 16 and 15). " For every high-priest taken from among men is ordained for men in the things that appertain to God that he may offer up gifts and sacrifices for sins : who can have compassion on them that are ignorant and that err ; because he himself also is compassed with infirmity" (Hebrews v. 1, 2). And our Priest Jesus in the days of His flesh, with a strong cry and tears offered up prayers and supplications to God, " and whereas indeed he was the Son of God, He learned obedience by the things which He suffered, and being consummated He became, to all that obey Him, the cause of eternal salvation" (Hebrews v. 8, 9). Jesus, our priest, like unto us, one of us, weak, tempted, in desolation, forsaken, persecuted like us, in order to learn all through experience of it and to compassionate more mercifully and more tenderly our temptations, our weaknesses, our miseries, our ignorances, and our falls, O Priest, loving and gentle, charitable and condescending, Priest of compassionate heart, may my confidence in always returning to Thee, without ever having any doubt of Thy heart, be my thanksgiving forever and ever.

III. Propitiation.

The view of the incomparable dignity of the priesthood of Jesus Christ enables us thoroughly to understand the crime which the world commits every time that by craft or force it combats the priests who, in the Church, visibly continue the priesthood of the Christ and become the real and visible personification here below of the Eternal Pontiff. However low may be his origin, however vulgar his mind, however limited his education, however common his virtues, from the moment that the most humble among the children of men has felt flowing into his soul some drops of the holy unction which consecrated Jesus Supreme Priest, and which from this adorable Head of the priesthood is diffused over even the lowest degrees of the sacerdotal hierarchy, that humble soul is a priest through the election of God, a priest through the communication of the priesthood of Jesus, a priest for eternity. He belongs to God, he is the property of God, His minister; he is His instrument, His organ, His mouth by which to speak His words and His law, His pardons and His condemnations; His arm to work the marvels of supernatural life, to create the realities of the sacrament, to apply the balm of it, and to distribute all the gifts of supernatural life. He bears in the profoundest depth of his being a unique and ineffaceable character. He inhabits the Holy of Holies, he is above all peoples, subjects, and kings, he belongs to God alone, he is the man of God. And unless a public apostasy causes him to be exiled from the sanctuary by the Church itself, he has a right to the absolute liberty of his divine ministry, to the respect, to the submission, to the humble and faithful co-operation of all. How, then, are to be characterized the attacks of the public powers against the rights, the liberty, even the vocation of the clergy? It is the greatest of social crimes, and it is committed against all the members of the hierarchy, from the child who is violently constrained to exchange the peace of the sanctuary, so necessary to his growing vocation, for the scandal of barracks, down to the Supreme Pontiff deprived of his liberty, and whose dignity is outraged by the usurpations of a sacrilegious power! But make reparation also for the prejudices, the miserable calculations, the injurious misunderstandings which influence but too many Christians in their practical judgment upon the priesthood; for the unreasonable oppositions, the disloyal, blind, and sacrilegious tyrannies, even in Christian families, against sacerdotal vocations. Lastly, if some star or other in falling from the firmament of the Church, causes grief to souls by the sound of its fall and dishonors the Church by its apostasy, make reparation still, by prayers, by tears, and by penance, for the crime committed by Lucifer in heaven and by Judas in the cenacle.

IV. Prayer.

Our Lord said to His disciples: "Behold how the harvests extend and are white; ask then the Master to send laborers to gather them in—*Rogate ergo Dominum messis ut mittat operarios in messem suam.*" May that be our ardent and urgent prayer when terminating this adoration. If the priesthood of Jesus is so beautiful, so powerful, so beneficent, if it be the necessary means of His mediation and consequently of the redemption of the world, ah! let us supplicate for innumerable souls the grace and the honor of participating in the priesthood of Jesus Christ, of spreading it, of multiplying it according to the exigencies of the glory of God, of the service of the Church, of the sanctification of men. Let us beg for priests, still more priests from Him who alone discerns, chooses, and calls them. Let us help by counsels, encouragements, and alms sacerdotal vocations, so thwarted in our days by the weakening of faith in families and by the spirit of evil animating the powers against the Christ and against His Church. Above all, let us not cease to ask for all priests a new and abundant effusion of the sacerdotal spirit of the Supreme Priest, the holiness of Jesus—that is to say, separation from the world and its spirit, the cordial and profound attachment to the God who is their sole portion in the Tabernacle, zeal for His interest in souls, and, lastly, the love which never recoils in presence of suffering, to complete in them the unbloody sacrifice which they offer every day and to co-operate thus in the redemption of the world—*Sacerdotes tui induantur justitiam et sancti tui exultent.*

THE SACRIFICE.

I. ADORATION.

THE most holy, most excellent, most powerful Priest, whose perfections you have seen and adored, must be contemplated by you now no longer in His person, but in His supreme sacerdotal office—the oblation of the sacrifice For although priests have different offices to fill in regard to God, and in regard to men, the most important, that which is at once the fundamental reason, the essential character, and the culminating point of their priesthood, is to offer public sacrifice to God. Sacrifice is in point of fact not the arbitrary homage of an individual, of a family, of a group. It is the religious homage of the great Christian family spread throughout the whole world. More than that, Christ having been consecrated priest in the name of all humanity, of which He is the head, His sacrifice is the solemn expression of the religion of all creatures, in all times and in all places. Behold, then, the adorable Pontiff clothed no longer in a linen robe, of dazzling whiteness, in a mitre of gold and a girdle of precious stones, but vested in the splendid clothing of divinity itself, and on which shine like costly embroideries all the varieties of the gifts, of the qualities, of the virtues, and of the merits of His holiness; behold Him ascending the altar to offer to God the sacrifice claimed at once by His supreme majesty, His inexhaustible liberality, and His justice injured by sin; behold Him rising from amid the multitude, greater and holier than all, bearing in His soul the responsibilities, the needs, and the desires of all. He is about to satisfy both God and men, to unite them together in a friendship equally worthy of God and necessary to the creature, to pay the debt of men, and to bring down the goodness of God, to present to God the sacred gifts of humanity and to bring to earth the sacred gifts of God.

But there is no sacrifice without a victim. Where is the victim of this Priest? It must be worthy of His priesthood. Priest infinite in dignity through the elevation of His divine person, it would be impossible for the earth to find for Him either in the fruits of its orchards or in the treasures of its mines, or in the beings which people it, a victim worthy of being placed in His thrice sacred hands and associated in His divine function. Be careful! Yes, the earth has found, it has given, its fruits—*Terra dedit fructum suum;* and this fruit has been accepted as very worthy of the divine Priest. But, again, where is it? Look attentively with the eyes of faith; it is only the light from on high which can enable you to discover it. Christ is a divine person possessing two natures, is He not? Well, this person, who is the Divine Word, God Himself, takes, seizes upon human nature, the soul and the body of Christ, His humanity in a word; He separates it from the corrupt mass of humanity in such a manner as to be absolutely ignorant of the stain of it; He sanctifies it, ornaments it with all graces, furnishes it with all powers; He attracts it to Himself, unites Himself with it, and penetrates it to the extent of becoming entirely one with it. In that union it becomes worthy of Him, holy with His holiness, strong with His strength, powerful with all His rights, agreeable to God, pleasing Him necessarily and fully as His Word, His own Son, the object of His eternal complaisance.

And then when He has chosen it, prepared and ornamented it, He takes it into His hands, presents and offers it to His Father, saying: "Father, Thou hast not wished the flesh of rams and of goats, but Thou hast made Me in body and hast asked Me to do Thy will; Thy chief will which is conformable to Thy rights is that the creature should render to Thee all its homage; it cannot do so aright except by annihilating itself before Thee, who alone merits to be, and in sacrificing itself to Thy majesty and justice; behold, I come —*Ecce venio!* Take, in the name of the whole creation, this body and this blood, which of themselves alone are worth more than all which ever issued from Thy hands; take them; may they belong to Thee, may they be immolated to Thee, and in their immolation may they give full satisfaction to all Thy rights and merit for Thy creature Thy pardon and Thy benefits!"

Behold, then, the humanity of Christ is the holy victim, of an infinite price, supremely worthy of the infinite Priest. The Person of the Word, which possesses all rights over this humanity because it is its Creator and its God, takes possession of it, consecrates it, and offers it as a holocaust.

Man, who owes himself to God in his double nature, which is both spiritual and corporal, having received both the one and the other from God, and having offended Him in both, will see himself redeemed by the sacrifice of the nature at once spiritual and corporal of Christ ; and God will be fully satisfied—*Christus et sacerdos et hostia. Ipse enim Dominus hostia omnium sacerdotum est, qui semetipsum pro omnium reconciliatione Patri libans, victima sacerdotii sui, et sacerdos suæ victimæ fuit* (St. Paulin. No. 1). Oh, do you understand the beauty, the grandeur, the depth of this mystery whereby Christ, the Priest, finds in Himself His victim, worthy of His priesthood, worthy of the God whom He has to satisfy, sufficient for all the requirements of the redemption of men ? Adore this holy victim with reverence and with love. But contemplate its immolation, and gratitude will then be united to admiration, producing in you the love which renders the admiration perfect.

II. Thanksgiving.

The Word accompanied the offering of His humanity to His Father as the victim of His sacrifice from the moment of the Incarnation, when He took it in the hands of His power. He keeps it before the eyes of His Father, as offered and immolated in His will and in His desire, during the thirty-three years of His life. And then the hour in which to immolate it really arrives. This immolation was performed in two acts, at two moments, and under two different forms. The bloody immolation of Calvary, in the face of Heaven, upon a hill as upon a high altar before the whole assembled people, with great splendor. The executioners were only the material and exterior instruments of the sacrifice in which the Supreme Priest immolated His body in the tearing open of the flesh and effusions of blood, and His soul in anguish, in terrors, humiliations, and abandonment. The sacrificer was the Divine Word, Christ Himself, who wished His immolation, permitted Himself to be consumed little by little through torments, but did not give Himself up to death until He deemed it well to do so, after all was consummated which He had to do here below; then He said in a low voice: "No one can take away My life, I lay it down when I will." Without this will of the Word, which delivered up His humanity even while remaining master of it to the end, neither the executioners would have been able to seize upon it, nor torments to attack it, nor death to vanquish it. This bloody immolation is known to Christians, nevertheless they will never be able sufficiently to bless it or even to understand sufficiently the love, the virtues, the heroism of it.

But there is another act of sacrifice which concurs in the immolation of the holy Victim, and which preceded the bloody act of Calvary; it is the immolation which took place at the Last Supper, the eve of the bloody death of the Christ. These were not two sacrifices foreign to each other, two distinct deaths of the holy Victim constituting two distinct sacrifices. Saint Paul teaches that "in His one sole sacrifice the Supreme Priest became the cause of eternal salvation." But this one sole sacrifice consisted in two parts, two acts—one at the Supper, the other on Calvary. The sacrifice of the Supper implied that of Calvary, and at the same time that it gave to the priesthood of the Christ its distinctive character it was destined to remain the permanent, continually renewed sacrifice of the New Testament. It is not according to the order of Aaron, by the bloody sacrifice, that Christ is a priest, but according to the order of Melchisedech, by the unbloody sacrifice of bread and wine. "*Mysterium nostrum,*" says Saint Jerome, "*in verbo ordinis significatur, nequaquam per Aaron irrationabilibus victimis immolandis, sed oblato pane et vino, id est corpore et sanguine Domini Jesu.*" Therefore the bloody sacrifice of Calvary, necessary for putting an end to the law of bloody sacrifices, by finishing their work of sanctification, which without this complement would have been totally inefficacious—the sacrifice of Calvary was instituted at the unbloody sacrifice of the Eucharist; it was intended to be only momentary, temporary, and to be terminated, to be finished, to become permanent in the wholly mystic immolation of the Eucharist.

Therefore there was, at the Last Supper, a true, real immolation, a true, real sacrifice—a sacrifice, be it said, once again, not foreign to that of the Calvary, but implying it, containing it, already executing it. Did not the Saviour say to His apostles, "This is My body which is given up, this is My blood which is shed for the remission of sins? *Corpus quod traditur; sanguis qui effunditur.*" It is as though He had said: "My humanity which I shall sacrifice to-morrow in a bloody manner, I sacrifice from this moment in an unbloody manner, by reducing it to be your bread, your drink; I destroy it, I pulverize it, I immolate it, and I annihilate it by rendering it capable of being eaten and drunk. And as the sacrifice of a victim has for its object the expiation of sin and the satisfaction of God, I

give thanks to My Father, I raise My eyes towards Him, I offer Him My life, I annihilate it beneath the sacramental species for His love, and this immolation will serve for the participating in the benefits of My Passion."
Is it not in very truth to be immolated and to die by becoming, from being a perfect man, a little bread? to assume the state, the conditions of it, full of abasement, by losing all which constitutes the state and the conditions of human life? Even as a corpse deprived by death of the life which animated it is no longer a man, but a thing, vile matter, so becoming, by the eucharistic immolation, the bread and the wine of the sacrifice, Christ is no longer the Man-God, the king of heaven and earth; He is the thing which we take, which we eat, which we drink, and whch is subjected to the humiliating conditions of matter. Now this sacrifice, this immolation, which Christ accomplished at the cenacle in person, He still accomplishes every day over the whole earth, from the rising to the setting of the sun, in the persons of His priests, who are only His visible forms, His instruments, and His organs. It is He who when saying by their mouth, "This is My body, this is My blood," immolates Himself by reconstituting Himself present under the appearances of bread and wine, by taking their condition at the price of all the prerogatives of His human glorified state. And that every day—everywhere—till the end! Without the ingratitude, the profanations, the inutility of His immolation in regard to a great number, making Him renounce the sacrifice of Himself for us with so much love that "having loved His own He resolved to love them to the end," and delivered up to them His holy humanity, His body, His blood, His soul, and His divinity, in sacrifice and for food, what thanksgiving

can be sufficiently large, sufficiently ardent, sufficiently humble and persevering to respond to the truth and the perpetuity of this sacrifice of our too loving Priest?

III. Propitiation.

Every sacrifice having as its object the confession by right and in fact of the supreme being of God and all His perfections, infinite like His being, ought to confess at the same time, and by a necessary correlation, the nothingness of the creature, the nothingness of his being and of all the qualities which it has; this double confession supposes a deliberate and voluntary abasement of the creature in presence of its Creator, a kind of free spoliation of itself and the surrender of all that it is into the hands and the disposal of Him who is its principle and its end. This righteous annihilation of that which is nothing through its origin and by its nature is expressed in purely spiritual creatures by a spiritual homage; but man being, at the same time, body and spirit, ought to interpret his internal religion by means of an exterior and material sign. Again, sin having deserved the chastisement of death, preceded by sufferings and accompanied by humiliation, the sacrifice which will have as its object the wresting away of man from condemnation, by appeasing the divine justice, ought, thenceforth, to accomplish through a bloody death, through a humiliating destruction, a violent death, submitted to as a chastisement, bringing with it the sufferings, the cries, and the natural resistance of the victim, the horrible effusion of its blood, lastly, its destruction and its consumption. In this manner man confesses his culpability, accepts his chastisement, and submits to it in the victim which represents him; and God, having received satisfaction, forgets the sin and grants forgiveness.

The sacrifice to be supreme must accomplish this law in its perfection. The adorable Priest will give up His humanity, which bore the weight of the sins of all men, to all the causes which can possibly destroy, consume, annihilate life; interiorily, the possessions of the soul, of the mind, and of the heart, joy, peace, tranquillity, affection, friendship, esteem, reputation, which are as the members of the spiritual being, were taken away from Him, cut off one after another; outrages after calumnies, abandonment after treacheries, condemnations after accusations, terrors, anguish, heart-breaking sorrow and heaviness seized His soul, devastated it, made it "*melt away and flow,*" leaving nothing spared; and exteriorly, the holy victim had been struck by so many blows, pierced by so many darts that He was nothing more from head to foot except one immense, deep wound, bleeding, hideous to see, covered with spittle and mud, all of which disfigured the Christ to such an extent that He had no longer the appearance of a human being. Behold the bloody, humiliating, ignominious death, merited by sin, and which the divine Priest had to impose upon His victim that His sacrifice might expiate the faults of man and pay his debt—*vulneratus est propter iniquitates nostras.*

This ignominious destruction of the Victim, a testimony of the acceptance of the chastisements deserved by sin, is necessarily inherent in the eucharistic sacrifice, because it is one with the sacrifice of Calvary; but with differences which distinguish the unbloody sacrifice according to the order of Melchisedech from the bloody sacrifice of the sons of Aaron. There are no more wounds in the flesh, no more visible effusion of blood, no more death by the violent separation of the soul from the body. But see how the victim is, nevertheless, destroyed, consumed, annihilated; on Calvary it was wounded, here it is crushed—*attritus est propter scelera nostra!* To be crushed is to lose form, extent, organization. The grain of wheat is crushed and becomes flour, a powder not having consistency, composed of almost imperceptible molecules—it is being in its most microscopic essence, almost without form, almost without extent, almost without quantity, without apparent action, without any well-determined place. Dust and nothingness are terms approximating to each other so nearly that they are commonly taken the one for the other.

Well, then, consider the action and the result of the eucharistic sacrifice. See it at the Last Supper; see it at the altar! The perfect Man, in the maturity of His thirty-three years, in the manly beauty of His features, in the full use of His senses, of His members, of His words, of His movements, of His liberty, what does He become there, in the hands of this same Christ who consecrates? A little bread, each crumb of which falls when the Saviour breaks it to give it to the Twelve, contains Himself in His entirety. Where, then, are His body, His limbs, His form, His human life? All has been compressed, crushed, reduced to this imperceptible particle. Christ is personally completely entire, completely alive in this dust, in this nothingness. Is it not the last degree of abasement, of humiliation, a real annihilation? But what is it that can sufficiently weigh down the Son of God in order to reduce Him to such powerlessness, to such weakness, to such degradation, to such death? Sin; the weight, the shame, the responsibility, the chastisement, and the expiation of sin! "Thou art dust, and unto dust thou shalt return," the Creator had said, trembling with anger against the revolt of man. And the Son of God made man, taking and bearing this chastisement, makes Himself dust and appears in this humiliated state before the eyes of the Supreme Judge whom He implores for the guilty.

This eucharistic immolation which was exercised at the Last Supper upon the mortal humanity of the holy Victim is exercised now upon His glorified humanity. It is another lower degree of annihilation. It is no longer only life and the human form, it is the life and the glorious form of His humanity upon which the divine Priest makes the sacrificial action weigh which reduces and crushes it until it becomes the fragile Host of our altars. What an incomprehensible and redoubtable power is that of the eucharistic sacrifice which is capable of bringing into, of compressing, of enclosing within the dust of our Hosts the glorified humanity of Him who is enthroned in the highest heavens in the full expansion of the most abundant, the most powerful, and the most beautiful of possible lives! Take a consecrated particle, escaped from the pious solicitude the priest exercises in gathering together the divine dust, and which remains forgotten upon the altar—where is the exquisite form, where the beauty, where the glory, where the splendor of Him whom you contemplate in the dreams of your hopes at the summit of the divine dwelling, worthy of attracting your eyes, of ravishing your heart, and of plunging you throughout eternity in an admiration which will be your beatitude? Examine, search, question! No, there is nothing which belongs to the man, still less to the glorious Christ! Obscurity, fragility, the vulgarity of the grain of dust; the atom, almost absolute nothingness; in any case the nothingness of the prerogatives, of the manifestations, and of the operations of human life.

Then place this particle, which contains the triumphant King, the Christ who has conquered the nations, and who has the most rigorous, actual, and immediate right to be honored, glorified, and exalted by the whole earth, in a tabernacle; let it be forgotten therein, let it be left there in poverty, forsaken, subjected to poverty, misery, solitude, and contempt; let it behold only the indifferent pass before it in the distance, and let those who approach it be only secret or public enemies; let it be touched by a sacrilegious hand, let it be profaned by being trodden under foot or cast into the filth of a contaminated soul, a true hell of which Satan is the recognized head and the king who is obeyed; the eucharistic victim will submit to all these privations, to all these degradations, to all these ignominies which complete the work of its immolation and bring it close to that which counts for nothing, to make it descend to what does not exist—dust and nothingness—*attritus est propter scelera nostra!*

Oh, how heavily sin weighs upon the perpetually annihilated Victim of the tabernacle! It is to expiate it that it embraces and accepts all these abasements which immolate it completely. But what an increased humiliation and suffering when, from the abyss wherein its love has cast it and keeps it for our salvation, it beholds us falling back into sin, and fearlessly persevering in evil ways, thereby rendering its immense sacrifices useless! We crucify it, we crush it anew, we bruise it still more ignominiously—*vulnus super vulnus addiderunt;* all the weight of its annihilation falls back heavily upon it then; it seems as though a sorrowful complaint issues from the bottom of the Tabernacle, saying: "My people, O My people, what ought I have done for thee which I have not done?" And its desolate heart, more crushed than all the rest, because it is the centre of misunderstood love, seems anew to experience the mortal heaviness of the agony : " Is it, then, in vain, without result and without fruit that I have sacrificed My heart to such a point! *Ergo sine causâ justificavi cor meum?*"

IV. Supplication.

The Victim of the sacrifice is offered to God for a fourfold reason—namely, to adore His supreme being, to appease His justice, to give thanks for His past graces, and to obtain new ones. This fourfold object of the sacrifice is attained in proportion to the personal qualities of the priest who offers it, and the value of the Victim which is immolated. In the eucharistic sacrifice Christ the Priest is infinite in dignity and in merit; His desires, His prayers, His personal action—all is infinite. It is the same with the Victim, penetrated with the divinity, its sufferings and its humiliations, the smallest drop of its blood and its slightest genuflection possess an infinite value, being, as they are, the fruit of the tree and the effects of the cause which are God Himself. What will it be then if this Priest-God immolates the divine Victim from the impulse of an infinite love for His Father and for men? what will it be if He immolates Himself through a sacrificatory action the most intense, the most extensive, the most painful, the most annihilating possible? what will it be, lastly, if He perpetuates the immolation throughout all ages and renews it at every moment of such duration not only in one place, but upon millions of altars at one and the same time?

This is, nevertheless, what takes place; it is what faith teaches! Our religion towards God, ours which is indigent and unworthy, ought, then, to rest faithfully upon the sacrifice of Jesus Christ; it is of value exactly in proportion as it identifies itself with that of this Priest and of this Victim equally adorable. It is our right and our duty as Christians to take part in this sacrifice, to unite ourselves with the prayers of this Priest, and to offer for ourselves and for others this Victim which suffices for the redemption of millions of worlds. Perhaps we do not sufficiently think of this honor and of this prerogative of Baptism which gives to every Christian a participation in the sacrifice of Jesus Christ, less extensive doubtless than that conferred by the sacrament of ordination, but nevertheless very real and certain.

This initial priesthood confers on us in a manner the power of sacrificing and gives us a corresponding right over the holy Victim. If we understood it aright we should render ourselves more worthy of this reflection of the sacerdotal dignity of the Christ which shines upon us; we should have greater confidence in resting our religion, our satisfactions, above all, our prayers upon the Victim of sweet odor, whose sacrifice is always accepted. We should pray more "by Jesus Christ, with Him, in Him;" we should draw near more often, "with fuller faith," to the altar where the holy Victim immolates itself. We should make the infinite price, the intrinsic value to be more enforced by representing to God its nature and its dignity; the perfection of its person and the virtues of its soul; the reality of its immolation and the depth of its annihilation; we should show it to Him stretched out and sacrificed actually upon all the altars of the whole earth, subjected every day to new and more atrocious ignominies which add to the radical sacrifice I know not what surplus and what superabundance; we should recall to God the engagements He took upon Himself towards it to hear it always and to give it all nations. This habitual intercourse with the holy Victim would penetrate us little by little, but every day more and more, with its dispositions, would unite us with its prayers, would enable us to enter, by means of mortification and humiliation lovingly embraced, into its immolation—victims with the Host we should place ourselves with it upon the altar of the sacrifice, accepting all sufferings, all humiliations, all privations, and all pains as the accomplishment of our sacrifice and the partial execution of our immolation; it would be perfect religion, the true Christian life, holiness. But also, at the hour when our sacrifice would be consummated by our death, our soul, loosened from all burdens, and free from all death, would rise straight to heaven like the perfumed cloud which ascends from the sacred charcoal in which the incense has been consumed.

Let us ask for ourselves, let us ask for all those whom we love and whose true happiness we desire, for our priests, above all, an abundant participation in the sacrifice of the holy Victim, in its spirit, in its fruits. Let us remember that when we communicate we eat a crucified flesh, a soul plunged in mortal heaviness, a victim sacrificed, in the very act of its immolation, in the state of its annihilation, and that all that renders it obligatory on us to make of our life a death in order that our death, on the last evening, should give us life without end!

The Eucharist a Memorial of the Passion.

I. ADORATION.

LET us adore our Saviour saying at the Last Supper, "Behold My body which is given up—*corpus quod traditur;* My blood which is shed—*sanguis qui effunditur.* Do this in memory of me—*hoc in mei memoriam facite!* Every time that you consecrate and that you eat My flesh and drink My blood, you will set forth My death—*quotiescumque . . . mortem Domini annuntiabitis.*"

Let us adore Jesus, instituting His Eucharist on the eve of His death, and causing to be merged together in one sole recital, by the evangelists, the event of His Passion with that of the Eucharist—*prius quam pateretur.*

Evidently our Lord created between the Eucharist and His Passion narrow and indissoluble links; and as the Eucharist is to perpetuate Himself here below, it will perpetuate itself there in its intimate alliance with the Passion and the death of the Saviour—it will be the authentic memorial of it, perfect and perpetual. The title of memorial which the Saviour gives it here—*in mei memoriam*—the Church will consecrate; it will be of divine institution, and will express one of the essential and sacramental ends of the Eucharist—*Deus qui nobis sub sacramento mirabili Passionis tuæ memoriam reliquisti.*

Adore this design of the Saviour, believe this truth, and as soon as you are in presence of the Eucharist behold Jesus appear, suffering and dying! Under the penalty of not responding to the intention of the august Institutor of the sacraments the sole name of the Eucharist ought to indicate the passion and death, even as the sacrament itself ought to contain the virtue, the work, the substance of the passion and of the death—*mortem Domini annuntiabitis!*

This act of faith marked out, the excellence, the superabundance, the rigorous exactitude the Eucharist joins Christ dying and dead to the risen Christ which it encloses.

Upon the altar, at the moment of the sacrifice, behold in what state the consecrating act constitutes Him—it is like unto the state of death.

The death of the Saviour consists in this that His soul, quitting His body, which is covered with wounds, disfigured, having little human about it, abandons it and leaves it inert and lifeless.

What, then, is this Host upon the altar? It is doubtless the living Christ; but in consequence of the state of bread and wine which He assumes do not the sacramental species deprive Him of all appearance of life, of all movement, of all action, of all liberty, giving Him up to the elements, to the will of man, like a corpse, and less even, since He has not even in them the features which recall the semblance of the man in His human remains?

The communion accentuates the signification of death, for it delivers Him up to us as nourishment. We are fed only with things which have lost their natural being, or which have been put to death, if there be in question aliments which have had life. Then, again, He consecrates us to lose His sacramental being, so frail nevertheless and possessed of so little life, but which at least gave Him a separate existence, an independent existence, a being of His own. He loses Himself and melts away in us; it is another step by which He descends into death.

His presence in the tabernacle by night and by day, being the continuation of the state of bread taken in the sacrifice, it simply perpetuates His state of death. And it is not for three days only, as it was in the tomb, it is for all ages. Ah, how He is sealed in a state like unto death!

All these significations which confirm one another, all these redoubled affirmations, ought to make us at once see in the Eucharist the passion and the death of the Saviour.

Behold the Saviour betrayed by Judas, condemned by Pilate, scourged and crowned with thorns by the soldiers, nailed upon the cross by the executioners, and dying abandoned by His Father; behold Him! It is He and not another!

It is Thyself, O Jesus! Faith tells me so; my heart makes me feel it; I cannot be one moment in Thy presence and ask myself who Thou art, without the state in which I see Thee telling me at once that Thou art the Man of Sorrows, the Divine Crucified!

It is a recital which teaches me; it is not a picture which recalls Him to my mind, it is Thou in person; Thou art there. It is this inertia, this silence, this form of a thing, and not of a human being, which continues in the only possible manner Thy death here below.

And it is Thou who, present beneath these signs of death acting spiritually upon my soul while the whole of this exterior acts upon my senses, sayest to me, criest out to me in a manner it is impossible for me not to hear it: "I am the Crucified! He who was agonized in the Garden of Olives, is I! He who was accused without defence, condemned without proofs, scourged, is I! It is I Myself who was thirsty, was betrayed, abandoned, insulted, mocked at, buffeted; it is Myself and not another! Where dost thou seek Him who died for thee, O soul, which cannot live except at the price of this death? Behold Me! Seek Me nowhere but in the sacrament; I am nowhere in reality except here; and all the signs of My sacrament are intended to make thee recognize thy Saviour suffering and dying. Dost thou not recognize Me? What, then, must I do that I may be recognized by thee? Is it My image or Myself that thou dost seek? Dost thou prefer it to the reality of My person? But, then, where is thy faith? The image of My death costs nothing, and it is insensible; but in order to continue the remembrance of My death for thee in the reality of My presence I was obliged to face, and I still endure immense sacrifices of which each one is worth a death!"

O Jesus! veiled beneath the Host, I recognize Thee as the Man of Sorrows, as the Crucified, as my Victim put to death on Calvary; with Mary, with Veronica, and the courageous women who followed Thee weeping, with Saint John and the good thief I adore Thee on the Calvary of the altar, the mountain of Thy sacrifice and of Thy death as really as the Calvary of Jerusalem. I make Thee honorable amends for having so often disowned Thee! Henceforth I shall know how to find Thee in Thy Eucharist, and therein to see Thy passion and Thy death, with all the love of the one and the other.

II. Thanksgiving.

Be Thou blest, O Jesus, who hast instituted so complete and living a memorial of Thy Passion, so efficacious and so powerful, so sweet and so attractive, so wisely conformable to Thy designs and to my needs!

Thy passion is my life for time and eternity. Outside faith in Thy death and the participation in Thy blood there is no eternal salvation for me, no pardon here below, no hope, no strength, no virtue, no consolation; everything is contained for us in Thy death, which alone has rendered us all that sin had made us lose. I have therefore need of Thy passion, it is requisite that I should participate in it abundantly, and that I should be able to have recourse to it abundantly, in all confidence and at every moment. Thou didst know these things, O Master, who hast thus regulated them in Thy sovereign omnipotence. And in order to make them reach me Thou hast instituted a thousand channels—prayer, the Gospel, the sacraments, Thy remembrance, holy pictures—and through all these means I receive graces, merciful results, encouragements, lessons, something, lastly, of Thy passion!

But even this was not enough! In the same way as Thou didst will to extend and to perpetuate Thy coming upon earth through the Incarnation, by remaining really, always present in the sacrament, so Thou didst will to extend to all men and to perpetuate throughout all ages Thy Redemption by continuing in person Thy passion and Thy death in the eucharistic state. And Thou hast been wise and good, foreseeing and condescending to our misery in this institution! For neither the Gospel nor the crucifix, nor any of the other means, would have been able to keep present to men in a sufficiently vivid manner the memory of Thy death. It was necessary that Thou shouldst continue to die Thyself every day before our eyes. And in spite of the sacrifices inherent to such a condition, in spite of the ignominies which would be inflicted on Thee, through it Thou hast given Thyself up to it, Thou hast remained on Thy cross, and Thou wilt remain there to the end, repeating to the world, without interruption, that Thou didst die for love of it, and for its salvation. O superabundance of the divine condescensions, be ye blessed!

I shall henceforth recognize my Saviour dead for me; I shall enjoy the sweetness of the love which flows with His blood from His mangled body, being, as it were, the juice of the grape trodden down in the wine-press; I will approach my thirsty lips to the living fountain which bursts forth from His transpierced heart. This Host suffered, was condemned, and put to death; and He already loved me then; and He loves me with the same love as that which He bore towards me on the cross, for it is the same death which He continues to endure for me, although under another appearance; whence can come the identity of the death faced and submitted to except from the identity of the love?

Without the Eucharist the passion does not say to me anything which is vivid enough—above all, loving enough; it does not apply to me the plenitude of the redemption and of its fruits, nor of its sweetness, nor of its love!

But Thy Host, O Christ, behold, that is the living, dramatic, complete, exact, touching, and sublime recital of Thy passion! Thy Host, behold therein my cross laden with its adorable Victim; behold therein my crucifix which keeps me, and everywhere, always, presents the Redeemer of my sins, which I weep over at His feet! And if the Real Presence shows me in so lively a manner the Crucified, the Mass, in renewing His death, accomplishes anew all justice and all salvation—God is as much adored, thanked, satisfied, and supplicated thereby.

And the communion brings me the Crucified, unites me corporeally to Him in a profound identity ; He is in me, and I am in Him, and I can then say, like Saint Paul, *Christo confixus sum cruci.* I am fastened to it, then, united, identified with it, not to the naked cross, but to Him who dies upon the cross. In coming to me, He applies to my soul, to my mind, to my heart, to my will, to each of my members and of my senses the virtues which He practised, the merits which He has acquired, the sanctifying efficacy gained by each one of His powers during His passion. Each communion is intended to make me die and bury myself with Jesus crucified. Happy tomb, whence I shall issue with Him on the day of my glory, when I shall have been remade by Him according to His eternal design ! Oh, what an undertaking ! The workman performs it on the spot, in person ; He works in us His own death, without the reproduction of which we cannot be saved, because those alone will rise with Him who will have died with Him !

Once more, O sweet Lamb, immolated every day, Thou art good, too good to us !

And as, although Thy death be necessary to us, Thou canst not really die, seeing that that is contrary to Thy risen state ; as, in addition, it would be too horrible a spectacle on earth to see a man put to death in blood upon all the points of the globe, Thou dost crown Thy goodness by dying a death which nevertheless leaves Thee living in Thyself, and in changing the act which immolates Thee and which was a crime upon Calvary into a most holy, most meritorious, and most sweet act for him who performs it. Instead of an executioner, it is a priest who adores Thee and who loves Thee; in immolating Thee, he sanctifies himself; and we—we can see all Thy passion unfold itself before our eyes, without feeling any terror caused by bloodshed, without hearing any cry from the holy Victim. My God, be Thou blessed equally in Thy wisdom and Thy goodness!

III. Reparation.

In virtue of the glorious state in which He is since His resurrection, Jesus is entirely exempt from all suffering of body and of soul, and can no longer die. It is of faith. Nevertheless the Eucharist (it is also an article of faith) is the memorial of His death. Is it a simple material memorial, a naked and insensible sign, like an inscription, or a monument which recalls to memory the death of a beloved being? No, certainly! Many, alas! believe that it is so, and on that account cannot in the least understand what is sweetest and most sanctifying in the Eucharist; they are ignorant in regard to it, of the form of the devotion and of the love the most capable of pleasing the God of the sacrament—compassion, the love of condolence, the sad and afflicted sympathy for the trials of a friend. Pardon me, divine Victim, for having hitherto misunderstood Thy eucharistic immolation and for being up to the present hour insensible to the new passion and the death to which Thou hast been subject since the Last Supper, and to which Thou wilt be subjected till the end upon the altar!

The Eucharist is not only a remembrance, it is the continuation of the passion of Jesus—the real, authentic, complete continuation, although under another form and in different conditions, of His passion and of His death.

Not being able to suffer after the manner of His mortal life, and yet desirous to continue His passion and His death by means of a real passion and death, although of a new kind, behold with what profound reality and with what touching heroism He does it! It is by constituting Himself in the conditions of bread and wine that He takes in order to become a sacrament and by accepting the really humiliating and sorrowful consequences for His heart, to which this state of an inert and common thing, without action and without life, exposes Him.

Firstly, the Eucharist permits of Him being reached direct in order to outrage Him; it is only there that He can be attacked in that manner; the species are chains which deliver Him up at the good pleasure of His enemies. Let it not be said that the species only are attacked, and that the living reality of which they are the covering cannot be struck! Did not the executioners who stripped the Saviour, those who spat in His face or dealt blows against His body, reach His heart to afflict it, His soul to fill it with suffering, His divinity to outrage it? The sacramental species are, to say the very least, the vestment of the eucharistic Christ. They are, however, more than that, they are an element of the sacramental Christ; for the Eucharist is composed of two inseparable elements—the substance of Jesus and the species of bread. Therefore it is the Host in its entirety, the Christ and the species containing Him which we adore with a sole worship of divine adoration. It will be the same when He is outraged, it will be Christ that will be attacked by maltreating and by despising the sacrament. Well, behold to what a condition Christ is reduced by His sacramental state: to the natural elements which decompose the Host; to the animals which can attack Him, soil and consume Him; to sacrileges and to profaners. What resistance can He offer to all these violences? Is not the Saviour subjected to the outrage of insults, of blasphemies, of public contempt, as in His Passion? Is He not therein outraged by His own, denied by the best, abandoned by all on certain occasions? Is He not cast on the ground in the bonds of His Host, pierced by swords, covered with spittle, buffeted with blows, trodden down and crushed under foot? Does He not groan in tabernacles which have become dungeons of ignominy for Him? Nailed in His Host and unable to come forth out of it, is He not therein devoured with thirst, deprived of the love of His own, which it would be so sweet to Him to receive? And is He not offered the gall of ingratitude, of harshness? Does He not still hear the arrogant challenges and the abominable provocations of His enemies triumphing over His silence and His powerlessness? And does He not in truth seem to be abandoned by God, by angels, and by men, when malefactors profane the adorable Host, soil it, mutilate it, and cast it into the midst of filth? Lastly, are not these species a heavy, cold, and sealed stone which loads Him with its ignominious weight, and which conceals His adorable face from the eyes of those who love Him and keep Him dependent on His enemies? Is not the sacramental state the death of the Saviour? You are right, it is a thousand times worse than death! Death snatches away the victim from his executioners, it is an end of suffering, it is in reality a deliverance. The sacramental state is death joined to life, weighing upon life, stifling life; it is the burial of a living being who continues to live, to feel, and to receive the outrages, the blows of hatred dealt Him by His infuriated enemies. O memorial of the passion and of the death of my Saviour, with what terrible reality Thou dost continue to recall them!

And having Thee before my eyes, perpetuating in reality Thy death for me, I could yet leave Thee to seek elsewhere a more speaking, a more efficacious remembrance of Thy redeeming love? O ignorance, stupidity, and hardness of my miserable heart! O man of little faith that I am! If my senses showed me a picture of Jesus suffering I should be touched, although it would be lifeless and loveless. Faith cries out to me that Jesus in person, devoured and consumed with love for me, is there in tortures and ignominies worse than those of His Passion; in a state more lamentable than that of His death; and the cry of my faith leaves me deaf, indifferent, insensible towards my Saviour Himself. Do not condemn me as I deserve to be, O merciful Victim of my miserable heart! On the contrary, give me the grace of a compassionate heart which understands how Thou hast substituted for Thy bloody passion Thy eucharistic passion, for Thy death on the cross annihilation upon the altar, in the bonds of dependence and the inertia of a material sign which delivers up Thy loving self to the indifference of Thy ungrateful creatures, glorious to the contempt of our pride, living to the evil treatment of the hatred of men and of the devil!

IV. Prayer.

The graces which we have to implore flow from the preceding considerations and from the resolutions to which they naturally give birth. The first resolution to be taken and the first favor to be asked for is assiduously to meditate upon the passion and the death of the Saviour before His memorial always present. We ought not to let a day pass without our doing so. Daily assistance at the holy Mass offers us the most favorable opportunities. It is the act which, in reality, accomplishes the renovation of the death of the Saviour. It displays before our eyes the divine memorial in all its actuality when at the words of the consecration the Christ invests Himself upon the altar with the state of bread and descends obediently, promptly, and silently into the sepulchre of the species wherein His love and the need of giving Himself up for us impel Him. Let us, then, recount the motives of the passion, the virtues shown by the Saviour in it, the ends which He pursues ; let us follow, step by step, each one of the circumstances of this drama of infinite love, the presence of the holy Victim, the renovation of His sacrifice, the virtues deposited in this sacrament, that He may infuse them in our souls, working in us, disposing us to enter into a communion of thoughts, of love, of generosity, of imitation of our Model. We shall enter into the wounds of Jesus, we shall penetrate into His heart, we shall descend into the deep and desolate regions of His soul, we shall assimilate ourselves to the passion, we shall finish by understanding it.

The first result for which we ought with joy to sacrifice all earthly happiness and to give our life a thousand times, we shall obtain much more surely still if we communicate sacramentally. It is the very object of the institution of the sacrament to reproduce in souls the efficacious remembrance of the passion of Jesus and of His death ; an efficacious remembrance—that is to say, living, active, fruitful, durable, making us really think, feel, and suffer as Jesus did, through the same causes and for the same ends. Now, can there be any better means for penetrating into the qualities of a thing than by feeding upon it ? We nourish ourselves with the flagellated and wounded flesh ; with the blood shed with pain in the effort of the agony, and flowing beneath the blows; of the heart frozen by ingratitude and treachery, torn by the apostasy of its friends; we nourish ourselves with the suffering and with the death, but also with the intrepidity of the flesh which resisted even unto the end; with the heroic love of the heart which loved to the very last; with the virtues, the strength, the patience, the meekness, and, finally, the love of that soul which always submitted itself, always gave itself up for God, because it willed His triumph, for us, because it willed our salvation. Ah, let us communicate in the passion of Jesus and in His death! Let us put our face on His wounded face, our heart on His desolate heart, our hand on His pierced hands; let us stretch ourselves out on this adorable Victim. And there let us unite our soul to His soul, let us lose it in the sorrows and the virtues, in the objects and the love of His great soul.

To communicate is indeed to do that—to enter into Jesus, to make ourselves one with Jesus, to identify ourselves with and to melt away in Him; but in Jesus suffering and dying, for it is there alone that is to be found the remedy for our vices, the destructions of our sins, healing, and life. Then, and above all, let us ask that grace of inestimable price, the grace of compassion, of sympathetic love, of heart-felt tenderness for Jesus suffering and dying; grace to love to meditate at length upon His sufferings, to return ceaselessly to Him; grace to know the secrets of the words which strengthen and raise up, and of those which console and soothe; the grace of holy tears, which, mingled with those of Mary and of Magdalen, soothe His wounds and seem to carry away in their torrents what is most poignant in suffering; lastly, grace to have our heart sufficiently pure and sufficiently loving, our soul sufficiently well disposed to draw near so closely and with such entire sincerity to our Saviour that He may pour upon us the overflow of His sufferings, pass a portion of them over to us, and so disburden Himself in some small degree of them. Therein consists perfect compassion " to attract to one's self the sufferings of one's friend" (Saint Francis de Sales), and enter into communion with His pains— "*In communionem ærumnarum venire*" (Saint John Chrysostom).

Ah, you may always bear within you a compassionate heart, touched, moved, wounded, and dropping with sorrow over the sufferings, the humiliations, the love of the dying Jesus! May you always have a soul so full of His sadness, of His abandonment, of His inmost griefs, as to find yourself utterly unfit for earthly laughter and joy! It would be then that you would always bear "upon your breast your Well-Beloved as a nosegay of myrrh, whose presence and perfume would give you immense strength to face sacrifice and mortification, and be the sweetest of consolations in the midst of trials and of desolation—*fasciculus myrrhæ dilectus meus mihi—inter ubera mea commorabitur.*"

Lastly, as all complete adoration calls for the homage of practical life—that is to say, of effective virtue, ask for grace and form the resolution to practise the great Christian duty of suffering, to keep in mind that we must suffer, not to fear suffering as the greatest of evils, not to be annoyed when it comes, to receive it as being detached from the cross of Jesus and passing through His heart; then to suffer it humbly, patiently, religiously, lovingly, in a very close union with our Head contemplated, received, assiduously supplicated; behold! herein is the grace of graces, perfect adoration—herein is holiness.

The Most Holy Body of Jesus.

Hoc est Corpus meum.
"This is My body."

I. ADORATION.

WHAT is the Eucharist?

It is the body, the blood, the soul, and the divinity of Our Lord Jesus Christ under the appearances of bread and wine. Make a precise act of faith, explicit and detailed, in the presence of the sacred body of Our Lord in the Most Holy Sacrament. His body is there united in it with His soul, living, organized, complete, filled with glory, immortal. It is the body formed of the most pure blood of the Virgin Mary, nourished with her milk, dead upon the cross, risen in glory, and which the saints behold resplendent in heaven. The blood of Jesus Christ flows in the veins of this body and maintains therein its life; it is the blood which comes from the most pure source of the heart of Mary, which was shed during the passion, and taken up again at the resurrection; it circulates in the body of Jesus and makes of it a living body. The eucharistic body of Jesus Christ is vivified by His heart, which really exists, moves, and beats in the Host. Believe in the reality of this body of flesh. It is not an image, but a fact; Jesus has said so—"*Hoc est Corpus meum;*" faith teaches it, believe it. And as this body is the body of Jesus inseparably united with the divine person of the Word, it is holy, sacred, adorable; adore it. Believe with all your strength in this reality; it is not a sign, a symbol, a remembrance, but the true body, the true flesh of Jesus. It is true that He is invisible, reduced to an imperceptible point; nevertheless it is there, whole and entire in the plenitude of its being, of its life, with all its members, all its organs, all its muscles, all its bones. It acts; we do not see its action; it is very real and very powerful. The eyes of Jesus behold us through the holy species; His ears hearken to our prayers; His head bears the impress of the crown of thorns glittering like a crown of diamonds; in His hands, in His feet, in His side, the marks of the nails and of the lance shine like rubies. Adore each one of the sacred members of the holy body of Jesus. Contemplate and kiss them one after another in spirit. The heart of Jesus animated with life in the Most Holy Sacrament is sensible of your love, of your attentions; even as your coldness, your irreverence in His presence afflict and pain Him, He feels them acutely. Believe, adore, revere, have a profound impression of this presence, a lively, durable impression, not an imaginative impression, for you will not be able to discover the manner in which Jesus is in the Most Holy Sacrament, but an impression born of faith. He is there, whole and entire, living, acting! I believe it!

II. ACT OF THANKSGIVING.

Thank Our Lord for His presence and for the great benefits which flow forth from it upon you. It is a real presence, sensible, at least by means of the species of bread which show it. Now, we need that an impression should be made on our senses, or otherwise we forget. It is the presence of that body which the patriarchs desired to see, after which crowds hastened ; we possess it, it is ours, it belongs to all, for all, always ! It is the presence of that body which by its sole contact cured so many desperate maladies ; the species are the powerful fringe of the vestment of Jesus ; He has as much of virtue and of power in His eucharistic as in His public life. And He works perhaps even more marvels, without our having any more idea of it. It is the presence of that body which at its death conquered Satan, reconciled the world to God, and opened forever the treasures of mercy. It has the same efficacy, works constantly the same effects ; give thanks, then ! It is true that it is veiled, but it is from condescension for your weakness ; we could not bear the splendor of its glory —it is another reason for giving thanks. And you have this body before your eyes, entirely yours ; is it not in it and through it that you have all good things ? Recall to yourself the temptations from which the reception of it in the communion have snatched you, the inveterate sins of which it has cured you, the strength and the consolations which it has procured for you ; ah, give thanks to the most holy, most excellent, most vivifying body of the sacramental Jesus !

III. Propitiation.

Make reparation ! for this body is forgotten, disowned, often even outraged ! Who is there that does not forget that the body of Jesus in the Eucharist has a true heart, a delicate heart, attentive, loving, really living ? Who is there that treats the Host as the body of God? as the living body, animated by Jesus in person?

Make reparation for heretics and console Jesus, for they say that the Host is only an image, a commemorative sign of the flesh of Jesus! They accuse it of falsehood! Infidels and rationalists say that the Eucharist is only a fable, an impossible superstition; what outrageous contempt! Bad Christians behave in its presence with a frivolity and a very contemptuous impropriety! And the good, and those who are dedicated to the ministry of the Eucharist, forget but too often when they approach the body of the Lord that His eyes are open, His person living, His heart sensitive, that He is, in a word, some one, a very worthy, very reverend, very adorable person.

Make reparation for yourselves, because these forgetfulnesses, these irreverences, these indelicacies are, if we look at them in a proper light, real crimes committed against the Divine Majesty. When we remember the honors, the homage, the adorations, the praises which the heavenly court render to this body of Jesus, and when we see the manner in which we treat it, we have indeed good reason to weep with grief and to tremble with fear. And I say nothing of the sacrilegious communions, the sacrilegious thefts, the horrible crimes committed against the most holy of bodies, crimes blacker than was the crime of the Jews, dragging along, flagellating, crucifying the body of Jesus! And this monstrosity takes place every day—yes, every day! Remember it! Live with this thought ever present to you, and if, after that, all your joys are not mingled with bitterness, it is because you do not know what it is to love Jesus!

IV. Prayer.

Pray, pray, then, to God the Father for the honor of His Son; ask Him to bestow upon us a more abundant grace of faith and love towards the eucharistic body of His adorable Son that He may be more intimately known, better treated, and more loved in the Most Holy Sacrament! Pray for the priests, the ministers of the altar, all employed in the Church, that they may always treat it with faith, reverence, and devotion! Pray for yourself and ask for the grace of a practical faith, sincere, constant, in the real and living presence of the sacred body of Jesus in the Eucharist. How quickly your life would change its aspect! How your prayers, your meditations, your piety, would be sanctified and elevated and become more profitable to you! Pray through the body of Jesus, through its passion of Calvary, through its heart, through its purity, its holiness, its mortification in the past; pray through its eucharistic annihilations, through its humiliations, its holiness, its separation from the world, its modesty, its sweetness in the sacrament; offer to God each of its members and the holy actions of each, and the thoughts, the desires, the love of its heart; offer its presence and all the services which it renders to God, all the homage which it offers Him, all the pleasure, the joy, the content, the glory of which it is the perpetual centre for Him.

Offer to God the body of His most dear Son Jesus by the hands of her who formed and nourished it for the salvation of the world; offer it as a reparation, as a wholly pure, wholly powerful prayer, a living and perpetual prayer, for the Holy Church, for your country, for all those who are dear to you, and for all your needs; the body of Jesus is salvation, surety, ransom, satisfaction, the superabundant price of all grace, of all benefits, of all succor; pray by the body of the eucharistic Jesus!

The Precious Blood.

Hic est Sanguis meus.
"This is My blood."

I. Adoration.

I BELIEVE with my whole heart and with the Catholic Church that the whole of Thy blood, O Jesus, my Saviour and my God, is contained and is present in the Most Holy Sacrament—present in Thy body hidden beneath the species, as in Thy body seated upon the heavenly throne; I believe that it is present and animated, living and glorified, circulating along Thy veins; real blood, human and divine together, human through its nature, divine through its union with the person of the Word.

I adore it as the blood of my God; I believe that each drop of it is united to the Word, immediately, without possible separation, and really deified by means of this marvellous contact and this ineffable assumption. I adore it and I contemplate it with the ecstasy springing from my faith in its splendor and in its beauty; it is a most pure blood, most ruddy, luminous, incorruptible, penetrated with the immutable and glorious life of the resurrection. I adore and I love it with the joy of my heart, for it is really human blood and of the same nature as mine; it is the blood taken from Mary, which flowed from her heart, which was fed and augmented by her milk, and which by means of a marvellous privilege of the love of the Son for His Mother always preserves the original perfume of its immaculate source. I adore and revere it with holy fear, for it is the blood of the immaculate Lamb, slain for my sins; it escaped from the veins of the Christ with immense suffering, and it covered the dust and the rocks of the grotto of the agony; it tinged the lashes of the flagellation and the thorns of the crown; it left its trace upon the pavement of the prætorium and on the streets of Jerusalem, upon the nails and upon the wood of the cross, upon the veil of Mary and upon the robes of Magdalen; the sacrament contains the whole blood shed for the love of man and for the expiation of his crimes. I adore it in the triple state which it puts on in the Eucharist; I believe that it is present in its totality in the host of the Tabernacle, therein animating the perpetual life of Jesus and making His five adorable wounds resplendent. I believe that it was shed under the distinct appearance of the wine at the sacrifice, thus reproducing the final act which separated it from the body of the Christ and inflicted death on the Saviour; but at the same time I believe it to be present under the one and the other appearance, inseparably united with the flesh of the Saviour and with His divinity. I believe, lastly, that it gives itself really and in its totality in the communion; I believe that it remains in the communicant in order to vivify, refresh, and render fruitful his supernatural life as long as the holy species last. Everywhere it is the veritable blood, most holy, most precious, most divine, of the Son of Mary and of the Son of God, the blood of the risen and glorified Saviour. To it be given adoration, praise, honor, and benediction!

II. Act of Thanksgiving.

Give thanks, be filled with admiring gratitude in presence of the bounties and the beneficent efficacies of the precious blood : all the effusions of these prodigalities are for us ; for us also and for our salvation all the marvellous effects of these all-powerful efficacies. Its prodigalities : it flowed at the very cradle beneath the knife of the circumcision, it was the impatient jet from a source which was about to overflow. It did indeed overflow during the passion—what channels were filled with its impetuous floods ! Blood from His face and from His whole body under the wine-press of the agony at Gethsemani ; blood from His forehead under the thorns of the crown ; blood from His shoulders beneath the leaded lashes of His flagellation ; blood from His hands and His feet beneath the point of the nails which fastened Him to the cross ; blood from His heart, exhausted to its last drop under the sword of the lance. And all this blood shed successively in so many ways till its complete exhaustion, it sheds itself entirely, mystically, and at one sole stroke in each one of the consecrated Hosts which cover the surface of the earth ! In all the chalices, every morning, at every hour of the day, in all the portions of the globe, it sheds itself anew ; it delivers itself up, it offers itself to the Father for me ! In my breast it sheds itself every day with all its plenitude, without cooling, without diminution or reserve ; and it is there in me, mine, for me ! And we are a thousand, a hundred thousand, who communicate every day ; and it multiplies its effusions that it may give itself to all ; in spite of that each one does not receive it the less fully, and all drink of the same chalice and slake their thirst and exhaust it down to its last drop. And of this blood, so lavishly shed, each atom is worth more than a world, and each smallest drop is capable of saving all mankind, of emptying purgatory, and of forming the happiness of heaven throughout all eternity. Ah! how can we sufficiently bless the royal, the divine bounties of the Precious Blood? And its marvellous efficacies, how can we describe them? how can we praise them sufficiently? It purifies; it is it which has washed the world from its crimes, and which purifies souls every day through flowing in them by all the sacraments, above all, by that of the Eucharist, for it is the wine of virginity. It fortifies; it is a generous wine, a wine which revives, an elixir of life; it brightens the faculties of the soul, sharpens the intelligence, strengthens the memory, warms the heart, and fills it with enthusiasm, ardor, generosity. It gives joy; it inebriates, it dilates the heart, chases away sorrow, dissipates sombre thought, and enlivens in discouragement, relieves despair—*dedit et tristibus sanguinis poculum!* It cures; it cicatrizes the wounds of sin, repairs the ravages caused by long-standing habits; it is an all-powerful balm for all the wounds of the soul. It is the milk of infants as well as the wine of the strong; it charms, it consoles, it is full of suavity and of delights. It is the pure and wholesome water, fresh and limpid, after which the thirsty stag and the weary traveller sigh; it appeases the fever of the blood, tempers the force of the passions, of anger, of voluptuousness, of covetousness; the soul drinks of it, bathes and plunges into it, and in it renews his life. Jesus, who hast deposited in the vivifying liquor of Thy precious blood all virtues, all savors, all balms, all inebriations and all charms, ah, be Thou blessed, thanked, glorified forever for this inexpressible gift! To Thy blood I owe my baptism; to Thy boold my First Communion and my daily communion, and the absolution which raises me up every time that I fall, and all these graces which forestall me, excite me, sustain me, enlightening my intelligence, strengthening my will; all the sap of my supernatural life, with the warm emanations which render it fruitful, the dews which refresh it, the succor which defends it, all comes to me from Thy adorable blood, shed once upon Calvary, shed every day mystically on the altar! To Thy blood I owe my heaven, and the sight of Thee, and Thy possession, and glory, and endless happiness! Ah! what shall I render to Thy blood for so many benefits? I will drink it and all the days of my life from the eucharistic chalice until I can drink it without interruption in the golden chalice of the eternal banquet!

III. Propitiation.

The effusions of Thy blood, O Jesus, my Saviour, so salutary and so beneficent for me, have always been for Thee, sweet Lamb, either full of suffering or full of humiliation—suffering during Thy life, humiliation in Thy Eucharist. If Thy blood flows beneath the iron of the circumcision, it is attended with painful suffering for Thy tender flesh of a little child. If it flows upon Gethsemani, in cold drops which soon form into rivulets on Thy body and on the ground where Thou dost agonize, it is the wine-press of anguish, of terror, of a mortal heaviness, which crushes Thee and makes it flow forth from Thy veins. In the prætorium it is the tearing open by more than three thousand blows of leaded lashes which rip up Thy body and discover Thy naked bones; but with what sufferings! And when the thorns go in search of it in Thy forehead and in all Thy adorable head, by piercing it through and through, what tortures endured in that centre of human sensitiveness! And when Thy knees were opened by striking the stones in the road against which Thou wert heavily cast by the weight of Thy cross, and the brutality of the soldiers and Thy own exhaustion! And when the nails pierced Thy hands and Thy feet, tearing the tissues, wrenching asunder the muscles and breaking the bones—what sufferings, what cruel tortures, what an assemblage of all kinds of suffering, of all kinds of torments! And yet it was far less the cruelty of Thy executioners which made Thy adorable blood flow than Thy love, which impelled it to pour itself out, carried away as Thou wert by Thy tenderness, Thy devotion towards us!

And now Thou dost still shed it mystically in the Eucharist. It is without suffering, but not without humiliation; it cannot be but that it must always cost Thee much to shed it and that its effusions must always be the effort of a love that is heroic and forgetful of itself even to immolation. It is humiliated by the annihilations of the eucharistic state, while in Thy glorious body in heaven it appears full of heat, of movement, and of life, coloring Thy cheeks, making Thy veins pulsate, manifesting itself by the thrilling joys of Thy heart, here it is veiled, reduced, silent, without appearance, destitute of life, incapable of affirming and of manifesting itself, it is deprived, moreover, of the essential quality of the blood which constitutes its value and its glory—that is to say, of vivifying human limbs and rendering them vigorous, active, alert, and resplendent with health. And, still more, on account of this annihilated state humiliation joins itself to humiliation to make it disowned and totally forgotten. How many of those who have a knowledge of the Eucharist think of therein adoring Thy precious blood, O Jesus, and of giving to it the worship of honor, of gratitude, and of love which it merits by so many titles? How many are distinctly aware of its presence, of its nature, its action, and its glorious qualities? And yet this precious blood is present in the sacred Host, and gives to it its salutary efficacies! What must be said of all those who, having deserted the path leading to the holy table, and having entirely forsaken the Eucharist, no longer render to Thy blood the worship which their Christian title and Thy rights as the Saviour make it an absolute duty for them to render? It is a fresh humiliation for this generous blood to be shed so often in our souls and so abundantly without succeeding in shaking off their apathy, in warming their coldness—in a word, without being able to make them live a supernatural life, active and generous, it is the humiliation of sterility for the most active principle of life! It is a humiliation which goes as far as insult, outrage, and ignominy, the humiliation to which Thy precious blood is subjected when it is received into sacrilegious hearts, when it comes in contact with their impure blood, in which ferment all kinds of corruption. Alas, I have greatly abused Thy blood, O Jesus, who dost shed it at the price of so many sufferings and humiliations! I have abused it and neglected it; I have not profited by it, and I have nullified its power; each one of my sins was an outrage committed against Thy adorable blood, a stain which I imprinted upon it, an ignominy which I imposed on it; and if I have communicated unworthily one single time I have rendered myself "guilty of the blood of the Lord," according to what Saint Paul asserts! I desire henceforth to make reparation by fleeing from sin, by the faithful and frequent reception of the communion, I desire to know and to honor Thy blood, to lend myself by means of a generous co-operation to the sanctifying work which it comes to perform in me. But there is still a very serious crime which is committed against the eucharistic blood of Jesus, and a very profound humiliation which springs from it; it is the adulteration of the wine destined for the holy sacrifice. Wine is especially the matter of the blood, it is immediately consecrated and changed into the blood of Christ, it is therefore a direct injury inflicted upon it when from avarice, interested calculations, or any other motive, an inferior wine, mixed or adulterated, is offered for the consecrating action. And in this age of a mercantile spirit carried to excess, where the public conscience is subjected to such profound attacks, how often is this crime not committed? Every soul which understands the price of the blood of Jesus will desire to make reparation for such a crime in so far as is possible to do so. As priests we will exercise the greatest care in the choice of the wine for the holy sacrifice; we shall desire that it should be always better and purer than what is used at our table; as simple laymen we will concur in this reparation by furnishing our priests, in proportion to our means, with an exceedingly pure wine, the fruit of our economy and of the sacrifices which we impose on ourselves to offer to the Lord this oblation of so agreeable an odor!

IV. SUPPLICATION.

"We pray Thee, O Lord, come to the help of Thy servants whom Thou hast redeemed by Thy precious blood: *Te ergo quæsumus, tuis famulis subveni, quos pretioso sanguine redemisti.*"

Let us pray, therefore, by the precious blood of Jesus—the blood of Jesus is a voice of mercy and pardon—*melius loquentis quam Abel;* it is the voice of the Pontiff and of the Supreme Mediator; a powerful voice, since it is the blood of the very Son of God; a voice which is not silent, for its wounds represent it always before the eyes of the Father; a voice which every day, at every moment of the day, utters aloud, when immolating itself at the Holy Sacrifice, a most solemn prayer, the prayer of the whole Christian people; a voice which comes from the heart of each man who receives the communion, and who can then present to God the blood of Jesus as being His own blood.

Ah, what a concert of prayer, perpetual, universal, ardent, humble, and sacrificed, issues from all the consecrated Hosts in each one of which the blood of Jesus prays, supplicates, intercedes, with all the love and the ardor of which it is capable!

Let us pray through the blood of Jesus; it is a ransom, and the price of all the virtues which we have to obtain. It has paid everything in advance and superabundantly; graces of conversion, of reformation, of light, of deliverance, graces to persevere and to advance, graces for life and graces for death; heaven itself and eternal glory, the precious blood of Jesus has acquired, gained, and paid for all this for us; and it is of a value infinitely superior to it all. Let us, then, offer and pay with this blood, for it is ours; its purity, its generosity, its intrinsic value, its sufferings, its humiliations—it places all in our hands; let us, then, make use of it with confidence!

Of ourselves we are nothing; with the blood of Jesus, everything!

Yes, we can, and we ought to offer the precious blood of Jesus enclosed in all the Hosts throughout the world, and, still more, the precious blood which animates the Hosts of our communions in order to glorify the Holy Trinity, rejoice heaven, the angels and the saints, to make the heart of Mary thrill with ever-renewed gladness; to succor purgatory, and to shed within it a clearer daylight of hope, and to deliver its dear prisoners; for the conversion of infidels over all the earth, for all the needs of the Holy Church, for all sinners; it is our right, our duty also, and under the penalty of burying the magnificent and inexhaustible talent which is confided to us we ought to accomplish it with the utmost fidelity and with the utmost confidence. Let us pray, then; let us intercede, let us pay through the blood of Jesus; it is the blood of victory, of redemption, of resurrection, and of life eternal!

The Heart of Jesus in the Eucharist.

I. Adoration.

"Once when the sacrament was exposed Jesus Christ, my sweet Master, presented Himself to me in dazzling glory, with His five wounds shining like five suns, and from this sacred humanity issued flames on all sides; but, above all, from His adorable breast, which was like to a furnace, and which having opened itself disclosed to me His most loving and amiable Heart, which was the living source of these flames."

Words of Blessed Margaret Mary.

Jesus, my Saviour and my God, truly and really present on this altar, permit me, I beseech Thee, to penetrate through the appearance of Thy sacrament to Thy adorable Heart. . . . Behold it! It animates Thy holy humanity which lives in the Eucharist; I have found it! Thou hast a Heart, O Sacrament of Jesus! It is Thy Heart which I will study and understand during this hour that I may praise Thee, adore Thee, love Thee more! O happiness, the Heart of Jesus is here, in its life, in its strength, in its love, in its beatitude! There, in the Host which reposes in the ciborium; there, in the Host which the priest divides at the sanctuary; there, in the Host which I received this morning at the holy table; there, lastly, Thou art in the Host which shines in the monstrance, O Most Holy Heart, and although my gaze is obstructed by the veil of the sacrament, my faith sees Thee, my heart feels Thee; I believe

Thee, I love Thee, I adore Thee present and living in this too amiable Eucharist, blessed sojourn of Thy presence, throne of Thy mercies, my Bethlehem, my Nazareth, my Thabor, my Cenacle, my Calvary, and my Heaven! I adore Thee, Heart really divine and really human, Thou art the Heart of Jesus, my God, and the Heart of Jesus, my Brother; two abysses of ineffable grandeur and of infinite loveliness!

Heart of Jesus, Son of the Eternal Father, Thou art united personally to the Second Person of the Holy Trinity; the Word possesses Thee, inhabits Thee, penetrates Thee, fills Thee; Thou art His Heart! This personal and loving union renders Thee all His forever, and renders Him all yours forever. Thou art the Heart of the Word, the Heart of God! By means of this union, so close and so profound, which death itself could not sever, Thou dost acquire all the greatness, all the perfection, all the power, all the rights of God Himself. Therefore I adore Thee, divine Heart of Jesus, majestic with the very majesty of God, holy with the very holiness of God, good with the very goodness of God, powerful with the very power of God. It is through Thee henceforth that we are loved by God; Thou art become the organ of infinite love, Heart of Jesus, Heart unique and beloved of the Father; Heart of Jesus, ardent Heart of the Holy Spirit and His chosen dwelling; Heart of Jesus, august sanctuary of the Holy Trinity; Heart of Jesus, Heart of God, I adore Thee, I adore Thee! I adore Thee with the adoration which is due to God alone; I love Thee with the supreme love which God alone merits; I praise Thee with all the praises with which God praises Himself in the concert of the August Trinity. And Thou are not less adorable, O truly human Heart, Heart of Jesus, Son of the Virgin Mary!

Thou art the most pre-eminent of hearts; all that God, in His wisdom and power, infused of what was great, good, strong, active, and intelligent into the heart of man, which He made the masterpiece of the most noble of His creatures, Thy Heart possesses in perfection; it is the ideal and the eternal type of the human heart in the double splendor of its nature and of its deification by grace.

Heart of Jesus, Thou hast been enriched, ever since Thy creation, with all the treasures of wisdom and of knowledge, with all graces and with all virtues. Thy knowledge unveils to Thee all the thoughts, all the intentions of men and angels; all the secrets of nature and all the mysteries of grace are open before Thee; I open to Thee my heart, which Thy knowledge has already penetrated; I desire that nothing should be hidden from Thee, O most vigilant Heart of my Master and of my Guide! All the praises, all the gifts, all the effusions of holiness exist in Thee in their plenitude; Thou art substantially sanctified, and the substance itself of holiness, O Heart of Jesus, my Model and my Sanctifier! And all virtues, all perfections, all heroisms, were practised by Thy Heart during its life for my salvation; and to-day, in the Eucharist, it gives me the grace of them; to-morrow, in heaven, their remembrance will be my joy and the theme of my praises. And Thy Heart was not created, or enriched, or sanctified, for itself alone; it is the universal cause of all virtue, the centre of supernatural life, and the very heart of the Church.

Every good inspiration comes from Thy Heart; every good movement has its primary origin in it, and it is from that source that it descends into our hearts. No act is virtuous and meritorious except through its union with the life, the virtue, the holiness of Thy Heart.

And when to Thy divine grandeurs and Thy human amiability thou dost add, by a surplus of love, the ineffable benefits of the Eucharist, Heart, infinitely sweet, of Jesus, I know not how to praise Thee, to bless Thee, and to love Thee enough! I therefore adore Thy eucharistic state. I believe that in the Host Thou dost enjoy the vision and the possession of God, without ceasing and without measure; but I also believe that Thou hast assumed therein a state and chosen conditions which condemn Thee to inexpressible annihilations; Thou dost veil Thyself, Thou dost enjoin silence upon everything which might otherwise manifest Thee; no longer any of those glances in which Thy goodness so sweetly shone; none of those words in which Thy mercy diffused itself so tenderly; no longer any of those sublime acts in which Thy love showed itself so victoriously, none of those marvels in which Thy power was displayed so magnificently; Thou hast enveloped Thyself in obscurity, silence, powerlessness; it is in this state that Thou dost give up Thyself to us in the sacrament, O Heart of Jesus! Ah, I shall know how to find Thee there, and, comprehending that this excess of humiliation is nothing but all excess of love, I will adore Thee more faithfully, I will sing of Thee more joyously, I will love Thee more cordially! To Thy Heart in the sacrament, to its greatness, its amiability, its presence, its love, be adoration, praise, honor, now and throughout eternity!

II. THANKSGIVING.

"On one occasion, being in presence of the Blessed Sacrament, I felt myself to be wholly invested with the divine presence, and our Lord said to me, 'My divine Heart is so full of passionate love for men that, not being able any longer to contain within itself the flames of its ardent charity, it is obliged to diffuse them, and to manifest itself to them that it may enrich them with its precious treasures."

Revelation to Blessed Margaret Mary.

The heart is made to love, and Thy Heart, O Jesus, the Heart which God willed to give to Himself, has never done anything since its first pulsation except to love, and to love me! The whole life of the Word Incarnate is nothing but love; but this love which, infinite from its first flames, seems nevertheless ever to increase in intensity, is Thy work, O Sacred Heart of Jesus! It is Thou who dost conceive it, who dost keep up its fire, Thou who dost incessantly impel its flame to issue from it; this love is Thee! In spite of shutting Thyself up in the breast of Jesus, covering Thyself with the mantle of the sacrament, surrounding Thyself with glory—in Thy mortal life, in the Eucharist, as in heaven, it is Thee I see, Thee I hear, Thee I feel in all that speaks, in all that is done, in all that is Jesus!

It is Thou, Sacred Heart, who didst shed in the mystery of Bethlehem, where incarnate love appeared for the first time, those charms so sweet, those attractions so powerful which captivate our hearts! Thou who didst give Thyself in the smiles and the embraces and the glances with which the infant recompenses his mother!

It is Thy Sacred Heart which accepted, which sanctified, and which rendered salutary to us the thirty years spent at Nazareth in obedience and work. It is Thy heart which conquered the devil in the desert, and our temptations in an act of love and adoration; it is Thy heart which didst multiply the bread to feed the hungry multitude; it is it which, affected at the sight of the mass of human misery, didst multiply miracles to succor it; it is Thy Heart which was touched by the tears of the widow of Naim and gave back to her her only son; it, which made Thee to be thrilled and weep with Mary Magdalen over the corpse of Lazarus; it, which moved Thee to tears over the hardness of heart of Thy country: Thy Heart loved so truly, so tenderly, so generously!

It is Thy Heart which made Thy passion and Thy death; it is it which delivered Thee up silent and meek to the kiss of Judas, to the blows and the lashes of the soldiers, to the condemnation of Pilate, to the ignominy and torture of the cross; and it is again it which inspired Thee before dying to pray for Thy executioners and to give us Mary to be our Mother! And in all the works founded by the Incarnate Word it is still love which is their object, and it is the Heart of Jesus which loves us! It loves us in the Church established for the life of the world, and of which it has made us children; it loves us in the Pope, to whom it has given the word of infallible truth and the power of limitless pardon. And I know that if, some day, the gates of heaven will open before me, it is to Thee that I shall owe it, most merciful Heart of Jesus, whose active and patient solicitude leads me, sustains me, and always brings me back. And in that sojourn of felicity what will be Thy heart if it be not still love? a love which satisfies itself fully and diffuses itself without measure.

Heart of Jesus! from Thy life and Thy death, from Thy Church and Thy throne, I receive nothing but love. But the focus of all this love, the flames of which vivify me, Thy Heart itself, wilt Thou not give it to me also? The wish is perhaps too daring, as I have already received so much? Ah, forgive me! but I cannot any longer repress the cry coming from my heart, " Give me Thy Heart, O Jesus, or else give me nothing! Thy love without Thy Heart would be an intolerable torment to me, for it would make me die of desire."

And Thou hast replied to me, " Take and eat, this is My body, this is My blood!" And the Eucharist has delivered up to me Thy Heart! I hold it, I possess it, I will not let it go! It is mine in the blessing of a real, universal, and perpetual presence, with all the virtues of its life and all the securities brought by the presence of the just, of the holy, of the Saviour! It is mine in the blessing of a sacrifice of infinite virtue which gives me every day all the satisfactions, all the merits, all the fruits of His passion and of His death. It is mine preeminently in the blessing of the communion which casts down the last barriers and delivers it up to me in its entirety! It is mine, I have received it, I have eaten it, it becomes myself! It awaits me, and its joy is to give itself to me!

And I came in the days of my innocence and I received the Heart of Jesus; and I came back after my wanderings, and the Heart of Jesus did not refuse to give itself to me! As long as I live I shall remember the joys of my First Communion; and I shall sing eternally the sweets of the banquet where Jesus rejoiced over my return. Heart of Jesus! it is Thou which wert the cause of the splendor and of the charms of the first; it is Thou which didst shed in the latter such an assurance of pardon that my soul, forgetting in it the miserable past, opened itself to hope and comprehended that it could live by love, since Thou didst love it! And the Heart which I then received I can receive daily, it is in truth mine! It is my daily bread, it is my life—in a word, my Heart, to sanctify me really and to lead me surely to the happiness which has no end; but Jesus, O Jesus! "what, then, is man that Thou shouldst visit him thus and set Thy Heart, as Thou dost, against his heart?"

III. Reparation.

"Blessed Margaret Mary being on her knees, with her eyes fixed on the tabernacle, Our Lord appeared to her on the altar, and, showing to her His heart, said, 'Behold this Heart, which has so loved men that it has spared nothing, but has exhausted and consumed itself to testify to them its love ; and instead of gratitude I received nothing from the majority except ingratitude manifested by their irreverence and sacrileges, and by the coldness and contempt they entertain for Me in this sacrament of love.'"
Revelation to Blessed Margaret Mary.

If the history of the benefits bestowed by the Heart of Jesus renders gratitude obligatory upon us, the spectacle of its sufferings is calculated to thrill us with love and compassion. From its dawn down to the hour on which it ceased to beat on Calvary, the life of the Heart of Jesus has been a martyrdom. God had created it to suffer, and has given it, at the same time as the mission of suffering, all the requisites for fulfilling it aright.

"Father," He said, when entering into the world, " Thou wishest no longer any victims of the law—behold Me !" The vision of His passion and of His future death, the sight of sin and of the forgetfulness of God, the triumph of falsehood, the adoration of Satan were as so many swords plunged from the very first into the Heart of Jesus, and which His zeal for justice made ever wider the wound. Rejected at Bethlehem, exiled to Egypt, disowned at Nazareth, His public life was constantly a prey to contradictions, to misconstructions, to calumny ; to come with open heart, with arms stretched out to embrace, and to see itself constantly disowned and expelled, what torture for the heart of a Saviour such as Thee, O Jesus !

Then came the passion preceded by the terrible agony. There Thou wast sorrowful, even unto death, O Heart of my Jesus, seized with fear, steeped in bitterness; there Thou didst make acquaintance with the nauseas of loathing and the faintness of discouragement! And the treachery of Judas, and the flight of the apostles, the denial of Peter, heaped their perfidious blows upon the Heart of the most faithful of friends! And the Heart which had never known anything but love heard the cries of hatred uttered against it. It met His Mother upon its path of ignominy, and this Heart of the most tender of sons was obliged to give her into the care of another! And when the whole world was against it its Father abandoned it; and beneath the pressure of this supreme sorrow it allowed its life to escape in a cry of anguish! And in order that it might be declared to all ages that it had died, overwhelmed with suffering and insults, a wretch, piercing it with a lance, engraved with an indelible stroke the last outrage inflicted upon a heart already pierced with so many pangs. After such sufferings and such ignominies was it not very just, O Heart of Jesus, that Thou shouldst forever enjoy felicity and glory? And, in fact, as soon as it resumed its pulsations on Easter morning it has never ceased to beat except to open itself with thrills of gladness, to receive the floods of delight which flow into it from beatific enjoyment. The career of physical suffering and of moral sadness is closed to it, and no longer in the Eucharist than in heaven can the Heart of Jesus suffer. Nevertheless His goodness on the one side, and our malice on the other, finds means of renewing a perpetual passion and death for the Blessed Sacrament—the passion and the death of humiliation and ingratitude. He chose for Himself through His love a state of annihilation and of subjection which occasions His Heart so many humiliations and so much opprobrium, that it is only He Himself that can reveal its depth to us : " Behold this Heart, which has so loved men that it spared nothing, even down to the exhausting and consuming of itself in order to testify to them its love, and instead of gratitude I receive from the majority nothing but ingratitude through their irreverences and sacrileges, and through the coldness and contempt they manifest to Me in this sacrament of love. And I feel it much more than anything which I suffered in My passion, whereas if they responded in some degree to My love I would esteem all I have done for them as being very little, and I would, if it were possible, do still more. But they give Me nothing but coldness and rebuffs in return for My ardor."

" Do thou at least," said Jesus to the confidant of His heart, " give Me the joy of compensating in so far as thou canst their ingratitude."

Sweet Saviour, in spite of my unworthiness, in spite of the share I have taken in the ingratitude which wounds Thee so cruelly, I will through Thy grace and Thy love console Thee and make reparation. I will make Thee honorable amends for the ignorance in which so many Christians are plunged with regard to the presence of Thy Sacred Heart in the Eucharist; they are determined not to know that Thou hast a heart therein, that it is a heart that is full of life and burning with love for them; and they treat Thee as an object which has no heart, entering Thy churches without showing any respect, remaining in them without feeling any piety, passing before Thee without making a genuflection, speaking, and insolently laughing ! And there is a still greater number of baptized individuals for whom Thou dost not even exist in the Eucharist, Thou whose heart watches over them, protects their life, and shields them from the blows of Divine Justice irritated against them on account of their apostasy. And among the good how many experience in the presence of Thy Heart the faith and the love which render a man pious and full of delicate, cordial, and religious attentions? Who is there that treats Thy heart as being the most sensitive and the most tender of hearts? I make Thee honorable amends for all the sins by which Thy heart is afflicted in the holy sacrifice of the Mass. So many Christians refuse to assist at Mass, even on Sundays, preferring to defile themselves with a mortal sin rather than give to Thy heart the satisfaction it would experience in heaping upon them the fruits of Thy death! And among those who assist at it how few think of Thy heart, of its agony, of its anguish, of the opprobrium to which it was subjected in the passion, of the abasement which it accepted in this sacrifice! But if there be bad priests who change themselves into executioners and who profit by the power they possess by holding Thee in their hands to insult Thee more closely, Heart of Jesus! who shall make reparation for the crime of such treachery, who shall console Thee for the shame of so cruel an hour?

I make Thee honorable amends for all the sins which outrage Thy Heart in the communion. Even there, in that juncture wherein it gives itself up so lovingly, what humiliations, what rebuffs, what treatment does not Thy heart receive! Pardon for all those who refuse this gift of Thy Heart on Easter Day! Pardon for those who neglect to receive it frequently when their holiness is the price of it! Pardon for the sacrilegious communions in which Thy most pure heart, condemned to come in contact with corrupt hearts, is subjected to shame worse than the kiss of Judas! Pardon for the lukewarm communions in which affection for venial sin, love of the world, cowardice in sacrifice, unite together to deprive Thee of the love of our hearts!

Lastly, I make reparation for the unworthy treatment to which the Host of Thy Heart is so often subjected! They touch it with their hands stained with theft, they hate it and they tread it under foot; they carry it away to their dens, true vestibules of hell, and it becomes the laughing-stock of their mockeries, the Victim of their diabolic rage; and even in these profaned Hosts Thy Heart, O Jesus, does not cease to live, to be silent and to love!

But, above all, pardon for our ingratitude which is the mother of all this coldness, of all these irreverences, and of all these crimes committed against the sacrament of Thy love; Thou dost love us, and we love Thee not; Thou dost feed us, and we despise Thee; Thou dost heap honors on us, and we turn Thee away by our conduct; Heart of Jesus, Thou art love, we are ingratitude!

IV. SUPPLICATION.

"I will give them all the graces necessary in their state. I will console them in their troubles. I will shed abundant blessings over all their undertakings. Sinners will find in my Heart the source and the infinite ocean of mercy. Lukewarm souls will become fervent. Priests will be endowed with the art of touching the most hardened hearts, and their ministry will produce, even in what has to do with the salvation and the perfection of each one of them, fruits beyond their hopes. My divine Heart will be a refuge during life, and principally at the hour of death." *Promises of the Sacred Heart.*

If there be a sentiment which springs spontaneously in the soul as soon as it becomes acquainted with Thy Heart, O Jesus, it is that of confidence. "My Heart will be there in the sanctuary," Thou hast said; "it will be there every day to listen to the prayer of all those who will come and pray in this place of My choice." And Thy Heart is in truth there!

It is the Heart of the Supreme Mediator which remains on the altar, between heaven and earth, in order to foresee our needs, to receive our prayers, and to carry them up to the throne of God : how would it be possible that this most holy Pontiff, who has paid with His blood for the graces He demands, should not be heard?

It is the heart of the very Author and of the sovereign Master of all blessings ; He can give freely, and as He will, and as much as He wills, and to whom He wills, for what He gives belongs to Him ; who, then, O Jesus, could fail to have confidence in Thy all-powerful Heart? It is the Heart of a Saviour whose mission is to solace all our sufferings, to relieve us in our miseries, to succor us in our needs, to pardon all our faults ; and that it might fulfil this mission perfectly it has been made of the same nature as our hearts, it has contracted the same obligations, experienced the same affections, felt the same pains, endured the same sufferings ; and all that in order to learn by experience to compassionate our infirmities and to make for Himself a Heart of indefatigable mercy!

Therefore it is the universal Heart, the Heart of all men, the Heart of the whole world ; it was opened on the cross, and it remains open in the Eucharist, that we may, all of us, enter into it. It is so large that all have their place in it, so vigilant that nothing takes place which it does not know, so sensitive that it seems to be the Heart of all, feeling within itself what all feel. It is upon these titles that I lean my prayer, O Jesus, and I know that Thou wilt not deny them. Heart of Jesus, Spouse of the Church, who hast loved her, even to the giving her birth in Thy open side, and who dost nourish her with Thy blood, give her peace; extend her empire, and give back to her her social authority over Christian nations! Heart of Jesus, eternal Pastor, who dost love Thy supreme Vicar, and who dost remain here below till the end to inspire and to sustain him, give back to the Pope the liberty of his ministry and of his States and preserve him long to our love!

Heart of Jesus, Bishop of our souls and source of the priesthood, who dost love Thy priests to such an extent as to give them the right to immolate Thee daily, give to bishops and to priests the zeal which makes Thee known and holiness which makes Thee loved! Heart of Jesus, Spouse of virgins and the first religious of Thy Father, who lovest religious so much as to dwell under their roof to give them the example and the grace of their holy state, I implore Thee for all religious; sanctify them in truth!

I pray to Thee for my parents and all my benefactors, Heart of Jesus, the most loving, the most grateful, and the best of sons! I pray to Thee for little children, and for young people who are about to face the dangers of life; preserve their innocence; vivify their faith, give them Christian courage, make Thyself loved by them, Heart of Jesus, Heart of a father, and Heart of a mother which engendered us in Thy death, which gave us to drink of Thy blood, and which dost follow us everywhere to defend us always!

I pray to Thee for all poor sinners, Heart of Jesus, Host of propitiation for their crimes, holy Victim which dost immolate Thyself every day upon the altar for their salvation!

I pray to Thee for all who weep, for the persecuted and the forsaken, most compassionate Heart, which has experienced the bitterness of tears, and which is so forsaken in Thy sacrament. I pray to Thee for our country; give it always a Christian government; protect all the institutions which serve Thee.

Heart of Jesus which lovest all souls, I pray to Thee for those who suffer in purgatory, and I offer Thee the merits of this adoration for their solace. I pray to Thee, lastly, for myself; my needs are immense; open to me the eyes of Thy Heart! Arm Thyself with patience; extend Thy goodness down to its last limits, be indulgent without measure! Heart of Jesus, it is only through Thy grace that I hope to be faithful to the duties of my profession; courageous in sacrifice, attached to the correction of my faults; patient under trials and persevering till the end in Thy love!

Grant to me, most beneficent Heart, always to remember that Thou art present and living for me in the Host; that Thou dost continue for me upon the altar Thy passion and Thy death, and that Thou wilt give Thyself really to me in the holy communion. I will therefore often receive Thee in it, and especially the first Friday of every month, according to Thy desire. And I will not be satisfied until I can truthfully cry out, "I have found my heart in Thy Heart—*Inveni cor meum ut orem Deum meum!* I have found Thy Heart to love Thee, Jesus; to love God, to love Mary, to love brethren, to pray, to labor, and to suffer; I have found Thy Heart in order to live as a Christian, as a saint, and in order to merit the life of eternal love!"

The Five Wounds.

I. Adoration.

The Truth of the Five Wounds.

WHAT are these wounds in the middle of Thy hands?

I believe, O Jesus, that Thou art the Christ, truly and really present in the sacrament. I believe that Thy hands and Thy feet and Thy sacred side bear, under the eucharistic veils, as in the glory of heaven, the sacred signs of the wounds which were inflicted on Thee at the hour of Thy passion by the nails and the lance. I embrace in spirit, I adore with faith, I consider with love, gratitude, and admiration these blessed stigmata, and I desire to fix the eyes of my soul upon them, to study them, and to comprehend the mystery of them. O Jesus, permit me to penetrate into Thy five wounds with Mary, Thy Mother, with Saint John, with Mary Magdalen, with Francis of Assisi, and with the saints of all ages who have loved Thee most tenderly and studied Thee most lovingly! Purify me, enlighten me, inflame me!

What, then, are Thy wounds? How were they inflicted on Thee?

The Saviour had ascended the slopes of Calvary, weighed down beneath the load of the cross, weakened by His three falls on the sorrowful way, clothed with a

mantle which adhered to the wounds furrowed by the
lashes on His shoulders, His head pierced all over by the
thorns of the crown, His cheeks torn by blows, covered
with mud and spittle, His eyes swollen with tears and
with blood. It is about noon. They divest Him of
His garments and tear the crown of thorns from His
head. Then the blood is seen oozing all at once from a
thousand sources ; strips of flesh came off with His vestments, and the august and holy Victim appears in a
humiliating nakedness before the curious, insulting,
and ferocious eyes of His executioners. This ignominious treatment makes His human flesh shudder beyond
all expression ; it is the height of insult and of indig-
nity. Then they present Him with a chalice full of
wine and gall ; Jesus tastes it in order to add this torment to all the others, and afterwards turns away His
head to show that He is aware of their sacrilegious
perfidy. The cross is on the ground ; they lay the
Saviour violently down upon it. Jesus allows them to
do what they will with Him, and with as much gentleness as the infant whom his mother puts into his
cradle. Silent and weak, His eyes fixed upon heaven,
he stretches Himself out on the cross like Isaac on his
funeral pile, and in giving Himself up into the hands of
His executioners it is to the love, to the justice, and to
the majesty of His Father that He abandons Himself !
Three holes had been made beforehand in the cross, two
for the hands, one for the feet. They take the right
hand of Jesus and place it against the right arm of the
cross ; opening the palm of His hand they fix a big,
long, and angular nail in it, and with a blow of the
hammer they drive it first into the flesh and then into
the wood of the cross. Blows are heard succeeding
upon blows, sometimes sharp, sometimes hollow, according as they fall upon the nail or strike the hand of the

Saviour. The muscles are torn, the nerves are broken, the flesh is crushed; the nail has gone through the hand and passed through the cross. Jesus continues His heroic silence, not an impatient movement, not a single complaint, His compassionate eyes are raised with infinite kindness towards His executioners, then fixed again upon heaven.

And He gives up His left hand. But it cannot reach the place which had been marked out for it. The violence of the crucifixion of the right hand had drawn the whole body to that side. The scene which followed was horrible. The executioners dragged the left arm with all their might, but they could not lengthen it sufficiently. They leaned their knees on the ribs which were cracked, but not broken by this violent pressure, and by dislocating the arm of Jesus they succeeded in stretching out the hand to its place. The horrible blows of the hammer again began to fall upon the hand, and their echo struck the hearts of Mary and the holy women, interrupted only by the blasphemies of the executioners and the satanic laughter of the Pharisees and the priests. The legs of Jesus were also stretched out with the same brutality; the whole was contracted by the barbarous tension of the arms and the knees were drawn up. The executioners fastened cords to the legs, and while some among them knelt on the breast lest it should yield to the effort and to prevent the hands, by tearing themselves entirely, from escaping from the nails which fastened them to the cross, others dragged the limbs brutally down until the feet were above the hole which had been made for them. It was a frightful dislocation. All the bones of Jesus cracked at one and the same moment, the protuberances and the articulations of the bones appeared through the skin. The sorrowful prophecy was then realized, "They have pierced

My hands and My feet, they have dislocated My body so that all My bones may be counted." The two feet being at last brought together were crossed and fastened one upon the other ; and through the solid mass of the shuddering muscles the nail was driven slowly, making Jesus suffer inexpressible agony, on account of want of fixity of the foot in this position.

They raised the cross and they placed it above the deep hole which had been made to receive it ; each concussion tore anew the hands and feet of the august Victim ; but all at once it fell with a rough and violent bound into the bottom of the cavity ; all the bones clashed against one another, His wounds were still more enlarged, and His blood flowed still more abundantly. These four great wounds open in the hands and the feet of Jesus were exposed to the burning sun without being dressed, during the three hours that He remained on the cross ; the perpendicular position of the body continued insensibly to widen them, each moment renewed the pain which had been caused by their having been opened.

Jesus has breathed His last sigh. A soldier approaches the cross, and with his lance pierces the breast in traversing the heart. On its being withdrawn a fountain of water and blood pour forth ; it falls upon the soldier, and is cast even upon the penitent thief as a salutary baptism. This wound is the last which Jesus received. He did not feel any pain from it, as His soul had already quitted His body ; but He had already accepted the ignominy of it, and had thus rendered it meritorious.

Tended carefully by Mary, by the holy women, and by Joseph of Arimathea, they were covered with the kisses of the Mother and of her companions and enveloped in spices ; they impressed their traces upon the shroud in which the body of Jesus was wrapped. On the morning of the Resurrection divine omnipotence healed them, put back in their places the bruised muscles, tied up the torn nerves and the wounded tissues, but it left the cicatrices clearly visible with a marvellously beautiful and graceful opening. And when Christ rose from the grave they ornaménted His hands, His feet, and His breast as the indelible marks of His victory. "Come, Thomas, put in thy finger hither and see My hands, and bring hither thy hand and put it into My side, and be not faithless, but believing" (John xx. 27).

When the full noon of the Ascension permitted the Saviour to cast away all the veils under which He held captive the glory of His body the five wounds appeared brilliant as suns. The angels hurried to His triumph; they vied with each other in exclaiming, "But what are these wounds in Thy hands?" And since they contemplate them with indescribable ecstasy, Mary, Joseph, and the saints adore and kiss them with rapture; Jesus keeps them as the trophies of His victory; He shows them to His Father as the proof of His love, as the sign of His obedience, as the price of the redemption, and as the ransom of all the elect.

On the Day of Judgment they will shine with revengeful splendor, and will make the wicked who will have despised the treasures of mercy which were offered by them for their salvation recoil with fear; they will be for the just the warrant of merciful judgment and of eternal benediction; then from eternity to eternity they will be sung, they will be adored, they will be blessed unto gladness. Meanwhile, every time that the words of consecration take their daring flight which nothing can arrest, that they may seize the living Lamb upon His throne, to constitute Him upon the altar in the state of His eucharistic immolation, the humanity of Christ, which exists whole and entire beneath the species with all its members, is there with its hands, its feet, and its side transpierced. The Host is the Host of the Five Wounds. He whom it contains is indeed Thee, O Jesus, who didst stretch forth Thy hands and Thy feet to the executioners who desired to pierce them; Thou who didst endure all the torments of the crucifixion, Thou who didst receive all the blows of hammers so cruel. It is Thou whose side was opened, whose side was transpierced by the lance. And Thou dost keep in Thy sacrament, in order to give me the fruit and the virtues of it, with the cicatrices and the traces of Thy wounds, all the love, all the patience, all the merits which Thou hadst when receiving them the first time. Jesus! Jesus! I adore Thy five wounds! I adore Thee on Calvary at the hour when Thou didst receive them; I adore them in heaven, jewels of Thy triumph; I adore them in the sacrament, the warrant of my salvation!

II. THANKSGIVING.

The Love of the Five Wounds.

"He was sacrificed because He willed it; like the lamb in the hands of the shearer. He was dumb, and did not open His mouth to complain." We are acquainted with the fact of the five wounds. We must contemplate their love that we may feed within our souls the sentiments of gratitude which this redoubtable but most sweet mystery calls for. Love, Thy love, when Thou didst allow Thy hands, Thy feet, and Thy side to be pierced, who could worthily comprehend it, O Jesus?

It is love which made Thee accept such torture. Certainly they had Thee in their power, they had bound Thee with cords; they had the superiority in numbers and in strength, but if Thou hadst not positively wished it, would they have been able to hold Thee for one single moment? Thou didst deliver Thyself up in greater degree than they took possession of Thee. It was Thy love which chained Thee. It was it that kept inactive the impatient legions of Thy angels ready to revenge Thee; it was it that restrained Thy power, Thy majesty, Thy holiness, and constrained all the rights of Thy divinity to be subject to the very end to such odious treatment. Each of the abominable acts of Thy executioners Thou didst will and accept freely and through love; to each blow of the hammer Thou didst respond by a fresh beat of Thy heart which said love, love on. And the suffering of each bruised muscle, of each broken nerve, of each drop of blood which flowed, Thou hadst clearly foreseen, individually accepted, and Thou didst accompany it all with the silent canticle of love which Thou didst chant in Thy Heart to Thy Father, and by the secret word of pardon which Thou didst shed upon us.

Executioners, strike, pierce, tear; beneath your winepress this ruddy grape sends forth without ceasing the purest, the warmest, the sweetest love! Open the hands which have had to labor so hard, the feet which have been so weary, and show to us the love which sustained and guided them, which rendered those hands so beneficent, those feet so beautiful, and so eager to hasten to the succor of all kinds of miseries! Open, open, above all, His breast and let us see displayed the Heart which animated this life, wholly spent in doing good, the focus of so much love and of so much tenderness, the centre of so many sublime and humble, strong and sweet virtues, at once so human and so divine! Thy wounds, O Jesus, are the great lesson of the love which suffers for those that it loves; the lesson of patience and suffering! It is the sight of them which sustained the martyrs in their torments.

It is the sight of them which alone can give supernatural patience in that other martyrdom to which we all are exposed, wounds, infirmities, sicknesses, with their necessary accompaniment of painful operations and of dressings more painful still, of insupportable remedies, and of humiliating subjection.

I suffer cruelly; my nerves are in a violent state of excitement; sharp crises become more frequent and prolonged; my wound is poisoned; I feel myself to be eaten away by ulcers; an inner fire consumes me, I am a prey to fever. How long are my days, and still longer my nights! I have passed years upon years in this torment; how much longer will it still last? Months, years, perhaps; perhaps always! O martyrdom! O poignant mystery! What! must I suffer, always suffer? It is hell already begun! What have I done to be so afflicted, and have I deserved it more than another?

To these terrible questions which my reason cannot solve, to these complaints which nothing here below can appease, ah, be blessed, a thousand times blessed, to have given the answer, O Jesus, by being the first to suffer through love of me! Thou hadst not in any way deserved to suffer. Thou mightest have satisfied the justice of Thy Father by a thousand other means known to Thy infinite wisdom, but Thou didst think of me; Thou knewest that I should have to suffer, and to undergo the tortures inflicted by iron and by fire in my limbs, and Thou didst will to set me an example and to encourage me. Heroic Jesus! with one sole stroke Thou hast gone farther into suffering than any human creature will ever go, and Thou hast borne more pain than all creatures put together will ever feel. What! hands and feet perforated, traversed by big nails driven in with a hammer, after the scourges had already lacerated Thy shoulders and laid bare Thy sides; after the thorns of the crown penetrating into Thy head and Thy brow had so profoundly attacked the centre of all sensation and of all pain! O Jesus! O Jesus! all that only for me! And in a body so delicate, so sensitive, in an organism so perfect! And all that without being soothed, without relief, without a drop of water having refreshed Thy lips, or a drop of oil softened the fire of Thy wounds, or a drop of wine having consolidated Thy flesh, or a dressing or a bandage having bound up Thy wounds, and stopped the blood, and kept together the throbbing flesh. Ah, let the whole multitude of wounded persons and of tortured criminals of all times and all places be united with me, all who are incurably devoured by cancers, ulcers, or gangrene, all those, lastly, who are suffering corporal torture, and them with me, and we cannot indeed but confess that our tortures are not comparable to Thine, and that in that one hour in which Thy hands and Thy feet were pierced Thou didst suffer more than we!

And it was without complaining, without showing any signs of revolt either against the pain or against the executioners who were torturing Thee or the friends who were forsaking Thee! And it was love which delivered Thee up to this torture, love which kept Thee there, love which closed Thy mouth against all complaints, and gave to the expression of Thine eyes such sweetness, such peace, such abandonment! Jesus, O Jesus, thanks! I possess the secret of my suffering, the remedy for my impatience, I have an answer surpassing my reason, and to the cries of my nature which faints. A glance at Thee is sufficient! If I still cry out, if I give way, at least let my hand in pressing Thy image, let my lips in pressing Thy wounds, let my eyes raised towards Thee, tell Thee that I accept all for Thee, and that my love utters the yes that triumphs over myself and over my pain, and which loves Thee in spite of all!

But these furrows in the hands and in the feet of Jesus are too deep to be nothing more than the characters engraved in this great lesson of patience in suffering. We do not cut even into granite so deeply! Executioners, what, then, are you doing, or, rather, love which forces them blindly to do Thy work, for what dost Thou still employ them? And love replies, "Pierce, drive still further in, enlarge, open the more. I will that these wounds should be a sanctuary and a citadel, an asylum and a refuge, a retreat and a dwelling, a harbor and a shelter. I will that they should be entered into, that they should be inhabited, that those who find their way into them should be at ease, that they should be sheltered in them, and that they should be able to hide and disappear entirely in them. Come to Me all ye who suffer, who are troubled, alarmed, tempted, accused, deceived, betrayed, calumniated, disowned, repelled, despised, in uncertainty, threatened, pursued, forsaken, overwhelmed, discouraged, rendered desperate; you whose eyes weep, whose hearts bleed, whose spirit is plunged into darkness, whose soul is steeped in bitterness, and whose life is ruined forever, you who can see nothing around you except frightful tempests or a silence still more terrible; you, whoever you may be, whatever may be your trouble and its duration, and its intensity and its cause, whether you have merited it by your sins, or whether it be sent to you as a trial, come to Me! Do not give way to despair, do not condemn yourselves, cease to descend into the abyss, or if the abyss calls to you inexorably, cast yourself into the abyss of My wounds and of My Heart! My Heart is open! I await you there with My hands dropping salutary balms; I will shed them upon your pains and your sorrows with attentions and a delicacy and a patience of which even the best of mothers is ignorant in regard to her infant, and the most charitable of physicians for his favorite patient!"

O words of life, of peace, of hope, and of salvation for my poor, guilty, and unhappy soul! But, Jesus, where art Thou? Is it at the Calvary of Jerusalem that Thou dost await me? Is it in heaven that I should seek Thy wounds in order to take refuge in them? Jesus, we are already so far from Calvary and still so far from heaven! Can we not find Thy wounds in the very place of our own sufferings and immediately beside us? And if it be only the blessed crucifix which presents to me the example and the grace and the refuge of Thy wounds, Jesus, ah! even this crucifix is only an image and a souvenir; something more is necessary to me— Thy wounds with the blood, with the love, Thy wounds with Thyself, Thou who hast suffered and who hast loved me! And love has foreseen this very desire and has satisfied this need of my heart. In the Host, under the sacramental veil, the Saviour keeps in His hands, in His feet, and in His side the wounds of His passion; they remain open, they continue to distil their balm composed of the blood, of the suffering, and of the love of Jesus, and they apply it to us. And these hosts are everywhere; they follow you, they surround you, and they press you; they are in very truth the Jesus who suffered for you, and it is Himself who reaches out to you, welcoming, hospitable, and sure, these retreats, these refuges so sacred and so sweet. Enter into them by the communion; you will penetrate more deeply into the wounds of Jesus by the communion than did the nails themselves and the lance of the centurion; you will enter into them more deeply than even Thomas. Kiss in spirit the threshold of these salutary retreats, let your mouth adhere to these veins of a water so limpid and so fresh; let these pure sources flow down upon you and cover you; bathe yourselves in these floods of life; cast upon your wounds the essence of these vermilion roses—in a word, repose in them and taste in them how sweet the Lord is! Make frequently, make daily, the consoling experience; only have faith and confidence; and bless with accents of real gratitude the Host of the Five Wounds, the Host of suffering accepted, willed, and borne by love; the Host in which the Saviour brings you all the examples, all the virtues of His suffering; the Host which will have bestowed on you patience and resignation, strength and hope; the Host which has suffered your own pains with you, in you, and more than you, uniting His wounds with your wounds, those of your limbs and those of your soul, to soften them, to sanctify them, and to render them fruitful.

III. Propitiation.

The Expiation of the Five Wounds.

"He has received these wounds on account of our iniquities; He has been wounded on account of our crimes."

It is Thy love, O Jesus, which accepts these wounds with their cruel sufferings, but it is sin which is the cause of them, and it is specially to expiate the sins committed by the hands, by the feet, and by the heart of man, that Thou didst receive these wounds in Thy hands, in Thy feet, in Thy heart.

It is therefore in the wounds of Thy hands that I ought to see the heinousness of the sins committed by my hands; it is in the wounds of Thy sacred feet that I shall comprehend the evil of the sins of which my feet were the instrument; it is in contemplating Thy heart opened by the lance that I shall understand the iniquity and the crimes of my heart; and it is the blood, the suffering, and the virtue of these wounds which will purify my actions, my thoughts, and my affections.

We have raised our hands in our foolish pride—*manus nostra excelsa;* we have said they are free from every yoke, they perform miracles of power, nothing arrests them, they pierce the mountains and annihilate space, it is the vote they cast into the urn which creates the authority of laws and that of the governor of the people —have we any other God to adore than the work of our hands? And because of the pride which man derives from the work of his hands, thine, O Jesus, which are the hands of God the Creator, the omnipotent hands, the hands which hold the reins of the government of worlds, are bound, garrotted, nailed down in powerlessness, in suffering, and in agony!

Your hands have taken pleasure in indolence; they are laden with jewels, with pearls, and with golden rings; they have triumphed in their delicacy and their whiteness, they have been an allurement to sin; bathed in perfumes they have languished in idleness, flying from the labor which might have interfered, in however small a degree, with their suppleness and beauty; but more than this, they have become impure, soiled, and criminal. And it is for that that Thine, O Jesus, Thy most pure hands, after having been bronzed and hardened during the hard labor of thirty years, are now wounded and torn; mud is mingled with blood upon them; and as their only jewel they bear the enormous nails which pierce them through and through.

The hands of men have been given up to violence; they have been the instruments of anger, of vengeance, and of murder. And in order to expiate these crimes and to wash away all the blood unjustly shed, Thy always gentle, beneficent, and healing hands, O Jesus, are struck, transpierced, and bleeding! Behold them under the tension of the crucifixion, stretched out, open, letting life, pardon, salvation flow liberally forth with their blood. It is to expiate the sin of avaricious hands which are always amassing and always remaining closed to the needs of the poor and the orphan!

They were fastened upon the wood by the unclean hands of the executioners. It is to expiate the crime of sacrilegious contacts, the crime of the hands of Judas, who was the first to touch unworthily Thy Eucharist, and of all those of his race who since Thou hast been in the sacrament have sacrilegiously touched, seized, and profaned Thee! Jesus! it is thus that in the suffering, the ignominy, and the transfixion of Thy hands Thou dost expiate all the crimes committed by the hands of man. Ah, let me kiss Thy transpierced hands; they stretch themselves out to my lips in the sacred Host; may I apply my hands to Thy hands in order to purify them; I ask of Thee pardon by the wound in Thy right hand and by the wound in Thy left hand, pardon for all the sins I have committed by my hands.

Thy feet, the prophet perceived them when he saw Thee come on the top of the mountains the herald of good tidings; he saw how beautiful and splendid they were, agile, strong, intrepid, indefatigable, fearing neither thorns nor briars, nor rough stones, braving cold and mire, sun and dust, sweat and weariness. They followed along the straight and right road, without ever turning away into the by-paths of iniquity; their footsteps mark the safe path, and he who follows in them does not walk in darkness. And now behold them covered with black and red mire, formed of dust and coagulated blood; they are deformed, torn, crushed horribly, perforated; they are nailed upon the cross, and they will everlasting preserve the stigmata of this hour of suffering and shame.

What is it, then, O Jesus? Thou wert obliged to expiate for the snares laid beneath the feet of the simple by the wicked; for the falls occasioned by stones of scandal deposited by the perverse under the feet of the innocent. Thou hast expiated for pride in the gait, and for the impatience which stamps haughtily with the foot—*apostata terit pede;* for the vanity which triumphs by an elegant style, by an agreeable form, by a lascivious grace; Thou hast expiated for all the steps, the attitudes, and the gestures in which voluptuousness and license find, at the domestic hearth as well as in public scenes, so abundant an aliment. All the steps, all the measures which the sinner takes in order to attain his ends, and each one of which renews his crime by renewing his resolution to commit it; all the wishes, all the desires, all the ardor he maintains that he may seize upon his prey, all the genuflections formerly performed before pagan idols, and all those which are claimed by the fleshly idols of a world which has again become pagan, and all those which, on the contrary, are refused to Thee in the temples where Thou dost nevertheless reside, Love of loves, Beauty of beauties, sole God really adorable—all these sins, all these stains, all these abominations of which the foot of man is the sign, the organ, and the instrument Thou hast willed to expiate, to take their chastisement, to pay their debts to the justice of our Father; and that is why, O gentle

Victim, Thy feet are bound, crucified, transpierced. Oh, how with Mary Magdalen and Mary, how with all the saints, I will kiss Thy feet and inundate them with my tears of repentance ! Jesus, by the wounds in Thy sacred feet which I venerate and lovingly kiss in Thy Eucharist, and of which the blood and the suffering flow into my soul by the communion as a remedy of life, Jesus, purify me, purify me !

If the feet and the hands are the instruments of so many sins, must it not be said that the heart participates in all the faults which man commits? Is it not the organ of the affections, and is it not the evil and ill-regulated affection for the creature and for material things which constitutes the essential malice of sin ? Therefore Thy Heart, O Jesus, began, for the sins of the heart, a secret expiation, from its formation in the womb of Mary ; therefore also it had its own passion on Gethsemani, where it was subjected in the anguish of sorrow, of fear, and of heaviness which reached even to agony, to the chastisement earned by the crimes of our hearts. But it was necessary that this passion should be manifested, and that the treasure of expiations amassed in Thy Heart should be shed ; that is why Thou didst permit that Thy side shouldst be pierced by the lance and Thy Heart opened ; two fountains immediately issued forth from it, and they will nevermore cease to flow ; they have formed two rivers of purity. The river of water flows in the baptismal fonts ; it washes the heart from its original stains and gives it its primitive purity ; the river of blood flows across the world in the sacred chalices of the altars, and it gives the active and meritorious purity, the purity which purifies itself every day more and more, and which at last becomes perfect purity.

Most pure Heart of Jesus, Thou art therefore pierced

in order to wash in this river of blood and of water our heavy, effeminate, and carnal hearts which have been intoxicated by the wine of sensual affection, and which having totally forgotten Thee, have perverted Thy best gifts! Spread, spread Thy purifying floods over our spoiled, depraved, and corrupted hearts, the burning centres of so much evil. Heart, most loving, the lance pierced Thee that Thy love, Thy condescension, Thy goodness, Thy generosity, flowing with Thy blood in these limpid and ruddy waves, should pay the ungrateful debt of our hearts, closed by selfishness, hardened by hatred, devoured by jealousy, insensible to the needs of others, and sensible only to their ruin in order to rejoice over it!

Most humble Heart of Jesus, the lance wounded Thee in order that Thy humility and Thy meekness might fall in floods, in order to move to repentance our proud, ambitious, insatiable, incredulous, mistrustful, hypocritical, perverse, and lying hearts, idolaters of themselves, and revolting against God, obstinate, hardened, and impenitent, established in evil and harder than granite.

For all these crimes, of which our hearts are the principal, the centre, and the means, I ask of Thee pardon, O pierced Heart of my Jesus, and offer Thee in expiation the anxieties, the anguish, the terror, the fear of Thy Heart, its sorrows and its loathings on Gethsemani, its sufferings and its agony on the cross, the deep wound which pierced it, the blood and the water which flowed from it! It is not by a simple desire, a pure fiction of my mind, it is in reality that I offer Thee, merciful Jesus, Thy own Heart in the eucharistic Host, wherein it lives always pierced; I offer it to Thee at the moment of its immolation upon the altar of the sacrifice; I offer it to Thee in its long annihilation in the perpetual tabernacle; I offer it to Thee in my soul when, having received it, I can unite and mingle my guilty heart with Thy innocent Heart, lose my heart in the gaping wound of Thy Heart, and say to Thee, "Pity, pity, for the sins of my heart, on account of the sufferings and humiliations of Thy Heart!"

IV. SUPPLICATION.

The Fruit of the Five Wounds.

"I will shed upon the house of David the spirit of prayer; and they shall turn and pray to Him whom they have pierced."

The fruits of the five wounds are innumerable; do not Thy five wounds sum up the whole of Thy Passion, O divine Lamb? Nevertheless they bear three principal fruits:

1. The power of prayer. Jesus had commenced from the moment of His coming into this world His office of Mediator and of Priest by praying without interruption. Still, heroic and sublime in all things, He willed to unite with the prayer of His desires the prayer of His sufferings; He made to Himself mouths of prayer throughout the whole of His body; to the voice of His sighs, of His cries, and of His tears He joined the voice of His blood, of His torn flesh, of His hands, and of His transpierced Heart; and it is this redoubled prayer which ended in conquering the justice of God and obtaining for us plenary pardon.

A Pontiff for all eternity, Christ continues in heaven His office of prayer, and it is by His wounds that He continues to pray. He shows them to His Father and calls on Him in our favor, summoning Him to bestow on the whole world all the gifts, all the succor which have been obtained for us by His wounds, His sufferings, His passion, and His death. Moreover, to add to this triumphant mediation the power of prayer anew humiliated, abased, annihilated, He descends again upon earth, He covers His glorious wounds with the obscurity and the infirmity of the sacrament, and God hears anew upon earth the prayer of the sacrifice and of the wounds of His well-beloved Son renewed in the abasements and the annihilations of the Host. But in coming here below to receive His ministry of prayer the Saviour wills to associate us in it; He comes to give purity, ardor, and force to our prayers by uniting them with His own. He is therefore there, in the sacrament, the Pontiff of universal prayer; He inspires, sustains, then gathers up and appropriates to Himself all our prayers, all our desires. He gathers them into the deep wounds of His hands; He plunges them into the still deeper wound of His Heart; there they are purified and become holy, fruitful, all-powerful; they participate in the prayer of the Supreme Pontiff, they acquire the virtue and the value of it; they become the prayer of Jesus Himself. O sweet mystery of intercession by the wounds of Jesus! Therefore it is that it will be by Thy wounds I shall henceforth pray, O divine Priest! I will present them to God, always open and supplicating in all the Hosts throughout the world. What, then, couldst Thou refuse me, Thou who hast said, "All that ye shall ask in My name of My Father, I will give it to you!" Well, I ask in Thy name, in Thy name of blood, written in Thy wounds on Calvary, in Thy name of power, shining in Thy wounds in heaven, in Thy name of love engraved in Thy wounds in the sacrament—Jesus, by Thy five wounds, hear me!

2. The apostolate of suffering. This is the second

fruit which the wounds of Jesus bear. Whoever suffers can, if he will—and it is his duty—co-operate in a degree of which God alone knows the extent, but which is always real and very great, in the salvation of the world ; continue the redemption begun on Calvary, and which will not terminate till the last day ; save souls, advance the reign of God, make that of Satan recede, help the laborers of God, sustain the Church upon earth in its combats, console the Church which suffers in purgatory, and enabling poor souls to leave it ; rejoice and glorify the Church in heaven ; for that end, and in order to labor very really and very efficaciously in all these good works, it suffices for him to unite his sufferings with the wounds of Jesus, and to suffer in union with the Saviour. This union is within the reach of all, it requires nothing that is difficult, the most ignorant among those who suffer can realize it. It requires first of all a state of grace and that the soul should be emptied of all mortal sin, for, in order to be united with the living Christ, it is necessary to be a living member ; but who is there that cannot with the help of the sacraments keep his soul in a state of grace? It is next necessary to draw closer together the union between our sufferings and His, our wounds and His wounds, by the communion made often, frequently, every day even ; therein lies the easiest, the sweetest, and also the most powerful means of strengthening the union. Then there is meditation, above all that which is made in the presence of the Host of the Five Wounds, in which the soul, while considering the sufferings of Jesus, finds therein strength to suffer, to accept, and even to love its own sufferings. The best means is to accept with resignation, through love for Him, through compassion for His sufferings, and even simply for the expiation of our sins and to merit paradise, the sufferings which it shall please Him to send us. The more this resignation is accepted with a view to Jesus and for His love, the closer it renders our union with Him. Therefore it should be impossible to renew too often the acts of it.

These, then, are all the conditions of the apostolate of suffering through the five wounds. Jesus, how easy Thy condescension has rendered them! That which happens then is sublime, magnificent! Jesus and the patient form one sole being, one sole person; the patient presents to Jesus the sufferings accepted by his members; Jesus pours forth the virtues and the infinite merits of His wounds; much more than this, Jesus appropriates to Himself these sufferings; the patient gives up to Him the members in which He incarnates Himself anew, and it is He who suffers with the patient, He who sanctifies, raises, and deifies His sufferings; Jesus then renews and extends His passion, and the passion of Jesus is complete satisfaction given to God, perfect peace given back to the earth.

Oh, all of ye who suffer, ye who are condemned to prolonged and perhaps incurable suffering, ah! accept it for the love of Jesus, unite it with the wounds of Jesus, unite yourselves with Jesus; suffer with Him, for Him, for His works, according to His designs and His desires, and you will perform, in your feebleness and your seeming uselessness, the work of Jesus, the work of the redemption; you will complete in your body, for His Church, what is wanting in His sufferings —that is to say, what, in order to be applied to them, awaits our voluntary co-operation.

3. Devotedness towards those who suffer. The third fruit of the five wounds is to inspire charity towards all who suffer, and to make nature love their wounds and overcome its repugnance in attending to them and dressing them, while consoling the unhappy persons who are

afflicted with them. O divine Crucified, before we had seen Thee torn, bleeding, like a leper, and no longer preserving the semblance of a human form, wounds, ulcers, leprosy, blood—in a word, were horrible and repulsive ! Woe to those who were attacked by these terrible plagues ! But since wounds are inflicted on Thee, since Thou art called a leper, the last of men, and a worm of the earth, and since beneath these wounds Thou hast been seen to attract the complaisant eyes of God and to excite the admiration of angels ; since, by means of these Thy wounds, Thou hast redeemed the world and cured the infinitely more frightful wounds of our souls ; since these Thy wounds were healed, transfigured by the glory of the resurrection, and since that the cicatrices which Thou hast willed to preserve shine like dazzling jewels in Thy hands and Thy feet—ah ! since that day human wounds have lost their horror ; they have become touching, worthy of pity, worthy even of envy ; and there have been seen those who were not afflicted by them regret it as being an honor and a happiness denied to them, and giving themselves, by way of compensation, to the dressing of wounds and the devoting of themselves to the wounded, to lepers, to those attacked by the plague, and to all who are a prey to suffering.

Divine Master, it is Thou who art beheld in these poor victims, Thou who art sought, Thou who art found there ! Thou hast been sought in the morning under the appearances of the sacrament, Thou art sought under the appearances of those who are sick, in order to continue the communion and to prolong the intercourse with Thee ; Thou hast given Thyself at the communion in the love, in the peace, in the inmost joys of the soul ; we feel the need of rendering Thee love for love in the service of Thy suffering members ; it is always the Real

Presence, always the communion, always Thee, O Man of sorrows, the Leper rejected by all, the Worm of the earth trodden under foot! The appearances which hide Thee in the sick are sometimes more obscure, more abject, more repulsive than those which veil Thee in the sacrament; but it is only an affair of appearances; faith reaches beyond them, love puts them aside, the heart discovers Thee, and it is Thee, nothing but Thee, that it then adores, Thee whom it loves and Thou whom it serves!

O Jesus, Jesus transpierced, give me, through Thy beautiful wounds, give to numberless souls to love Thee sufficiently, to believe firmly enough in Thee that, adoring Thee and receiving Thee at first in the most sweet sacrament of Thy wounds, they may give themselves up afterwards with generosity and with fidelity to this ministry—a ministry unutterably sublime and sanctifying, of the poor who are wounded, of the poor who are crippled, of the poor who have ulcers, of poor lepers, of poor incurables, for love of Thee, for love of the Church and through charity for those suffering, wounded, and transpierced members of Thy sacred body!

The Eucharistic State.

I. ADORATION.

*The Annihilation.**

Vere tu es Deus absconditus, Deus Israel Salvator (Is. xlv. 15).
"Thou art truly a hidden God, O God the Saviour of Israel."

ADORE Our Lord, really present, God and Man in the Blessed Sacrament, and supplicate Him to permit you to study, to comprehend, and to honor the state which He has chosen in order to remain there with us. It is a veiled, hidden, annihilated state; Jesus is hidden in it, not only from the intellect, but also from the senses; and this kind of being abases and humiliates Him; it is not accidental and temporary, but stable and permanent, inalienable; it constitutes the foundation of the sacramental state and the principle whence flow all the consequences of that state, as well in regard to Our Lord as to ourselves.

Adore the mysterious state; contemplate it! It is

---

* Saint Paul has entitled annihilation—*exinanivit semetipsum*—the human state of the Word. Cardinal Franzelin gives us in his admirable "Treatise on the Eucharist" two testimonies of Saint Gregory of Nyssa and of Saint Cyril, in which the eucharistic state is called by the same name, *exinanitio*, and he shows that it is the term which is the most suitable for designating the state of the Incarnate Word in the Eucharist.

composed of several elements which concur together not only to render more profound and more complete the annihilation to which Our Lord reduces Himself in it, but also to show the greatness of the love which leads Him thus to annihilate Himself, and the necessity of the virtue of humility, the guarantee of all the others, of which He gives thereby the imperishable and striking lesson. The eucharistic annihilation is, first of all, obscurity; the sacred Host which has nothing brilliant about it hides the glory with which the holy humanity of the risen Christ shines in heaven and with which it ought also to shine here below. It is, moreover, the absence of form which annihilates the ravishing beauty of the face, of the demeanor, of the whole humanity of Jesus; the sacred Host presents only the exterior appearance of a little bread, a very common thing, without any attractions for the eyes, and so generally diffused that it does not attract any attention.

Next, it is inaction, inertia, powerlessness, the privation of everything which makes up, shows, and manifests life; there is neither sensibility nor movement, nor a glance of the eyes, nor words, nor exterior action; none of the usages, none of the relations of life; but dependence, the inert passivity of matter. Lastly, it is a state of death, of burial; yes, Jesus is there buried deeply, covered, disappeared; He is less apparent than the human corpse which preserves in its features a vestige of life; and the sacred species do not even bear a sign, a name which permits of a distinction between the Host which is consecrated and that which is not, as we distinguish an unhallowed stone in a necropolis from the stone which covers mortal remains.

Like unto death, the state of death. Behold then the sum total of what constitutes the eucharistic annihilation of the Saviour; could there be a veil that was thicker, a deeper retreat, a more impenetrable mystery? There are caverns which succeed one another in the side of certain mountains and which plunge into unimaginable depths, rendering the night which reigns in them more and more terrible; in the same way the Lord, the Most High, seems never to be sufficiently in retirement, sufficiently abased, sufficiently hidden, sufficiently annihilated, and He adds silence to obscurity, inertia to obliteration, powerlessness to dependence, in order to hide and to annihilate Himself the more.

Such is the eucharistic state, the sacramental annihilation. And this state, freely chosen by the Saviour, meditated upon throughout eternity in His wisdom, the masterpiece of His omnipotence, which, in order to realize it, had to multiply prodigies—this state was assumed by Jesus from love; He has espoused it forever; He loves it, it will last as long as the Eucharist, and that in spite of the scandal of many, in spite of the abuse which human malice will wreak against it in order to forget what is due to this hidden God, or else to insult Him therein more freely. Ah, you, at least, adore Him! Know how to recognize in this humiliating state your Saviour and your God; confess Him, praise Him, say to Him with all the love of which you are capable: "O God, my Saviour, Thou art really a hidden God; I confess and adore Thee as my God! Under this obscurity I adore Thy majesty and Thy glory; under this simple and common appearance, the most beautiful of the children of men, and the face which ravished the angels; under this inaction the activity of the creative God and of the Providence which rules the world; under this powerlessness the very power of the Incarnate Word to whom has been given all power in heaven and on earth; under this aspect of death the full and perfect life of the divinity and of the persons of the adorable

Trinity; the life of the soul, of the body, and of the heart of Jesus, the active, anxious, ardent, eager, loving life of the Pontiff who prays without ceasing, of the Advocate who pleads for us, of the Head of the Church who rules and protects it, of the Father and of the Saviour of our souls; lastly, O Jesus, I adore in this annihilation, I adore Him who is all!"

II. THANKSGIVING.

The Work of Love.

Dilexit me et tradidit seipsum pro me (Gal. ii. 20).
"He loved me and gave Himself up for me."

The Eucharist being the supreme masterpiece of the love of Jesus, and each of its marvels, of its applications, of its manifestations being an act of love, we must attribute without hesitation to the love, and, moreover, the love the most powerful of the Saviour, this marvel of His eucharistic annihilation, the foundation of the whole of the sacrament. What, then, is the design of Thy love, O hidden God, in annihilating Thyself under the veil of the species of bread? It is that I will to be with thee everywhere, with the rich and the poor, with the laborer in the fields as well as with the citizen, on this continent and on the other, everywhere where there are men to help, to protect, to console; could I be so if I were not to take a state which takes up so little room, which renders Me so small, which requires so little that the smallest space suffices for Me, and that the poorest of tabernacles does not form too pronounced a contrast with My destitution?

I desire that thou shouldst have confidence in Me,

that thou shouldst dare to approach Me, to pray to Me, to speak to Me fearlessly ; I desire not only thy respect, but thy friendship ; I desire to become familiar to thee, as the brother is with his brother, the child with its mother ; much more than this, I desire that thy sins themselves, thy former sins and those which still stain thee, should not prevent thee from having recourse to Me, to obtain the grace of forgiveness ; should I obtain it, and wouldst thou dare to do it, if I were to appear to thee in the splendor of My majesty, in the radiance of My holiness, with the flaming eyes of the Sovereign Judge surrounded by the legions of angels who accompany the King of heaven and of earth ?

I thank Thee, O hidden God, who hast pity on my timidity and dost provide so paternally for my good !

I desire to be the Victim perpetually immolated for thy sins, a Victim which renews the expiation as often and in as many places as sin is renewed in ; I desire that the sacrifice should be as obstinate, the pardon as obstinate as the offence is obstinate and the hatred obstinate ; I desire that the fountain opened on Calvary should never be dried up, and that its floods, poured forth continually beneath the action of the sacrifice, should cause the mire of crime to be submerged, and should cover the world with a perpetual flux of grace and of salvation.

But what priest would dare to immolate Me in order to continue the sacrifice of My death if he were obliged ostensibly and with the sensible effusion of My blood to renew My cruel passion ? Who would dare to ascend the Calvary where I desire to attract to Me all men, to purify them in My blood, if he were obliged to assist at those frightful scenes in which My flesh would be flagellated, torn, crucified, and where the blood would stream forth from My hands and My feet transpierced ?

Nevertheless this sacrifice is necessary for thee ; it is

requisite that thou shouldst assist at it, and that thou shouldst keep under My cross and offer Me as a Victim to My Father. Thou dost shudder? My love has been the means of conciliating everything together; I shall die, but the species will hide My death and will veil the effusion of My blood; I shall be thy Victim, but so hidden from the eyes of thy fastidiousness that My sacrifice will be the most touching and the most attractive of the feasts at which the child himself will take pleasure in assisting without feeling any distress.

Be Thou blessed, O hidden God, who knowest so well how to ally the necessities of Thy justice with the exigencies of my weakness!

I desire to be thy food and thy drink. In order to maintain the divine life which I gave thee at baptism, it has need of a divine aliment; to become like to God it is necessary that thou shouldst be nourished with God; I am the God made man whom thou must eat. Yes, it is requisite that thou shouldst receive Me in person, and that thou shouldst eat My flesh and drink My blood, which will give thee My soul and its virtues, My divinity and its perfections; draw near and eat— *propera et manduca.*

Wherefore hesitate? Thou art troubled and drawest back? Ah! thou darest not eat My bleeding flesh, dip thy lips in the purple flood which escapes from My veins? Thou art horrified and takest fright, crying out like the men of Capharnaum, "It is too hard! Who, then, can eat human flesh and drink blood?"

Alas, in taking flight thou dost fly from life! But look at it more closely. I have made Myself bread! My flesh and My blood, My whole body, I have reduced, bruised, kneaded into a morsel of bread. Behold, it is indeed bread; taste, it is bread; eat fearlessly, it is the bread of thy heart, that which children eat, artisans and the poor, daily bread! Take with confidence and eat with joy! Meanwhile, I will spread throughout the whole of thy being, I will be diffused therein, together with My substance, My virtues, My qualities, My morals, My perfections. I will nourish thee truly with Myself.

Hidden God, I now comprehend Thy annihilations! Thou lovest me! Thou lovest me too much! Thou desirest to possess me, to do me good, to heap Thy love upon me, to give Thyself to me, and to raise me to Thee! Thy majesty, Thy greatness, my earthly state, my weakness, my prejudices, everything is an obstacle! But Thy love has triumphed over Thy majesty and my lowliness, and it has made of Thee such a one, by annihilating Thee beneath this veil of bread, that I find Thee therein even as I have need therein to possess Thee, present without my timidity being scared, immolated without my being affrighted by the solemnities of death, eaten without my teeth crushing anything except a savory bread!

There are abasements to be submitted to; they are for Thee! The profits are for me! Thus doth Thy love will it, and Thou never dost resist Thy love!

III. PROPITIATION.

Excess.

Quis credidit auditui nostro? . . . *Vidimus eum et non erat aspectus*. . . . *Unde nec reputavimus eum!* (Isa. lIII. 1-3.)

"Who will believe it? We have seen Him without form and without the appearance; His face was disfigured; He appeared to us as the last of beings, and we would not even think anything of Him."

The state which the eucharistic veil creates for Jesus is indeed a state of humiliation, of weakness, and of dependence; it is like unto annihilation itself. But as He assumes this state only through love for men, for the sake of their good, and for their advantage, men ought doubtless, from gratitude, apply themselves to the raising up again, in so far as they can, their God, dragged down for them into such an annihilation! Love, honor, respect, eagerness, triumph, they will desire to manifest that they may exalt Him and to re-create for Him in their love a glory, a throne, a court, a kingdom. It will be an admirable strife between the love of God abasing the Divine Majesty in favor of man, and the love of man raising up again the God who was abased Himself!

Alas! alas! Would it be possible to believe it if one did not know that fallen man is capable of all kinds of baseness, of all iniquities, of all species of cruelty, even the most monstrous? If we did not know that sin is synonymous with stupidity, ingratitude, hardness, and that it makes the heart to be lost at the same time as the senses?

Will the veil which Jesus casts with such great love over His majesty serve for anything else but to make Him to be still more disowned and despised? The weakness which He embraces to-day will be a pretext for abusing Him! There will be added to the humiliations of His state outrages and shameful treatment; and Jesus, who has already placed Himself so low, will find Himself driven back to a still lower degree through our contempt, our ingratitude, our hatred! And thus this primary excess of love which dragged Him down into the depths of the sacrament will only have been the means of hollowing out an abyss, more profound and more horrible, into which man will precipitate Him beneath the weight of his ingratitude. Deep calleth unto deep! The abyss of the voluntary humiliations of the Saviour will call unto the abyss of the humiliations of ungrateful, hardened man!

What a subject of compassion for the divine annihilated One of the tabernacle!

And if love had foreseen these abasements, far more difficult of acceptation than the first were, would life and all eternity be too much for the understanding of such love and for making some return for it? Now behold what a surplus of humiliations the ingratitude of man adds to the humiliations of the eucharistic state embraced so generously by the love of the Saviour. Because He is obscure, devoid of splendors and of dignity, He is forgotten, no account is taken of Him, He is treated disrespectfully, without attention; we are in His presence, and we are distracted, wearied, we yawn, we sleep, we think of everything else except Him; we allow our thoughts, our eyes to wander over creatures, and how many times do we not thus and seriously offend Him, even at the very moment when we ought to come only to honor Him?

Oh, if He were but to show Himself resplendent in glory, if His angels were to appear at His side! But, no, He confides Himself to our love; and our love disowns and despises Him. Because the eucharistic veil deprives Him of speech, of strength, and of action, because He cannot either defend Himself or take flight, or call for help, He becomes the play of the elements to which negligence abandons Him, and of the treatment inflicted by the hatred which pursues Him.

Hatred will join with negligence in assaulting this conquered, this powerless, this annihilated victim of love. Must it not weigh down with humiliations upon humiliations the shoulders of the Most High so generously abased through love, and must it not cuff and cover with spittle this face of the thrice holy God, whose eyes are closed by love?

The impious, the freemason, the thief, the sacrilegious man, all profaners can seize upon Him, carry Him away, make use of Him for their sacrilegious comedies and for their rage; He will be stricken, soiled with spittle, trodden under foot, bruised, crushed, cast into filth. And yet it will be He, always He, nevertheless, He in this mire, He in these ignominies!

But in order that it should be thus it was requisite that He should assume the eucharistic state; He foresaw this surplus, this most bitter of dregs which our hatred was destined to pour into His chalice, this excess of abasement in annihilation itself! Go, traverse the whole earth, draw near to all the tabernacles, reverentially open all the ciboriums in which the abandoned Hosts sigh; follow that which the wicked profane, and offer them your tears, your love, and your consolations!

IV. Prayer.

Fruit of the Host.

Hoc sentite in vobis quod et in Christo Jesu, qui cum in formâ Dei esset, . . . semetipsum exinanivit (Phil. ii. 5-7).

"Let this mind be in you which was also in Christ Jesus, Who being in the form of God . . . emptied Himself for your love."

The eucharistic annihilation of Jesus is the root of all the virtues of which He wills to give us the lesson and the perpetual example in His Eucharist. The Eucharist has as its object to continue not only the presence of the Son of God upon the earth, but His teachings and His example. Now, it is upon the state of annihilation that rest and live all the other states which we may consider in the eucharistic state—the state of poverty and obedience, the state of patience and of meekness, the state of chastity and of devotedness. Without the annihilation which reduces Jesus to be the sacred Host, to take the state, freely to accept and to keep through love the conditions and the consequences of that state, all these virtues would immediately cease to be so visibly, so perseveringly, so amiably taught us.

But there is one greatest virtue of all which results from the eucharistic annihilation, which flows from it, which is the flower of it, the fruit, the aroma, the splendor, the beam, the necessary consequence, a virtue so intimately connected with this state that it is one with it; that virtue is humility.

Humility is the primary and the immediate emanation of the eucharistic state; we cannot look at the Host without seeing in it the Son of God abased in presence of His Father through love, renouncing His rights through love, subject to man through love, so humble in all respects and in all ways that humility seems as though it were the sole thing at which He had aimed when taking on Himself the eucharistic state. Therefore, after love, the love of God and of our neighbor, there is no virtue which communion tends to produce more directly and more fully in the soul than humility.

Therefore it is humility above all which is taught by the contemplation and the adoration of the sacred Host. Hence, it is the sacrifice and the reparation of humility which the Saviour offers above all to His Father through His sacramental state, and which He opposes to the furious and universal overflow of human pride. Pray, then, supplicate Jesus to reproduce in you the dominant and essential virtue of His eucharistic state; ought not humility to be the dominant and essential virtue of your holiness, and ought you not to consider it as a primary principle without which all the other virtues would be useless; in such a manner that it enters into all your virtues as the predominant portion of them, into all the duties of your state, into your whole moral and spiritual life? It is because it is the fundamental and necessary virtue, it is also because pride is the principle, the cause, and an integral part of all our sins that the Saviour wills by His eucharistic permanent and visible state to teach, above all, humility, and by the communion to give the grace and the strength to it more abundantly than to every other virtue.

Beg of Him, therefore, to make the virtue of this sacramental annihilation act upon you, ask of Him humility and the other accessory virtues which live by humility, protect and develop it.

Extend over yourself the veil which covers the Christ in the Eucharist, by silence respecting yourself, your actions, your merits; veil yourself with the modesty of your demeanor, of your manners; veil yourself by performing simply and obscurely your duty, by rendering services and devoting yourself to others without affectation. Annihilate yourself by thinking little of yourself, by keeping down all thought of, all complaisance in the excellence of your mind and of your heart, in your more or less remarkable qualities.

Descend ever deeper into the depths wherein you will meet the annihilated Christ, by sincerely despising yourself, by practising all your duties, by following all the inspirations of humility, by obeying, by disclosing yourself to your guides, by accepting to be directed, led in all things, to be abased and raised, serving for all things, like the Host; by accepting to be discussed, judged, calumniated, condemned like the sacred Host, like the hidden God Himself!

Lastly, and still like the Host, accept, bring down

Thy heart in spite of the superhuman severity of the sacrifice, accept to be disowned, betrayed, forsaken, even by those who are dearest to you, even by those to whom you have done the most good ; like it subjugating yourself always, yielding always, willing absolutely and without reserve, but sincerely and courageously, to be nothing in everything and everywhere ; arrived at this point you will be one with it, you will live in it ; it will be suffering and total death, yes ! but it will be the perfect way and perfect happiness ! The veil which annihilates Jesus and delivers Him up to the malice of men, renders Him, at the same time, invulnerable and withdraws Him into the joy and the glory of His Father ; this veil will cover you also ; leaving all that you are humanly to humiliation and suffering, you will live in the joy and in the glory of Jesus, in His peace and in His love, in His Heart and in His Host.

The Diffusion of the Eucharist.

EVERYWHERE!

I. Adoration.

Ponam tabernaculum meum in medio vestri, et non abjiciet vos anima mea. Ambulabo inter vos et ero Deus vester, vosque eritis populus meus (Lev. xxvi. 11, 12).

"I will place My tent in the midst of yours, and My heart will never be weary of you. I will walk among you, I will be your God, and you shall be My people."

YOUR God, your Saviour, light, succor, pardon, consolation, Jesus in the sacrament, is before your eyes, opposite you; you have only had, in order to find Him, a few steps to take; perhaps your door touches His, perhaps you live under the same roof! Neither seas to cross over, nor mountains to climb, nor obstacles to vanquish, nor distance to traverse; He is there! His being so near, you owe to the great mystery and to the still greater love of the eucharistic diffusion. Adore therefore our Lord, saying, "*Ecce, ego vobiscum sum!*" Oh, what does it mean? With us? But we shall be everywhere in the two hemispheres! Well, I will be with you wherever you may be. And that is what takes place.

Contemplate the fact, the realization of this magnificent promise, and see if our Lord be not sacramentally everywhere—in Europe, in Asia, in America, in Africa, in Oceanica. And it is not in the capitals of the nations or in the large cities that He only resides, it is in every town and in every village, in hundreds and thousands of places at one and the same time in the same country.

Adore Him in all these tabernacles, in that of Saint Peter in Rome, in that of Nôtre Dame in Paris, in the tabernacles of all our basilicas and of all our cathedrals. Adore Him in the oratory where the Supreme Pontiff comes to invoke and to consult Him respecting the government of the Church; in the church of the humblest village where the priest comes alone to offer Him his homage and to solicit His help for His ungrateful sheep; in the poor hut of the missionary where He is his strength, his consolation, the one friend who speaks his language and understands him; adore Him carried in haste to the dying in their agony, reposing upon the poor table in the garret, then upon the lips of the dying man whose last sigh He sanctifies; adore Him upon the altar when thousands of priests consecrate Him, on the holy table when hungry multitudes come to receive Him; adore Him every place that He is, even to the particle which lies unseen and hardly appears at the bottom of the ciborium! Everywhere it is He! the Sacrament, Jesus!

Praise and admire the divine power of the Saviour who works the unheard-of miracle of multiplying His presence in the Host in so wonderful a manner; the simultaneous presence of one and the same body in several places distant from one another is one of the greatest miracles which can be performed; and this miracle includes a great number of others.

Adore the divine immensity of which the Host, diffusing itself everywhere, always remaining the same, without division or separation, gives the clearest and truest idea. Is it not of the universal presence of the Eucharist that it may also be said, " Lord, where can I fly from Thy face ? *Quo a facie tua fugiam?* If I mount the highest summits Thou art there in Thy best beloved sanctuaries—*si ascendero in cœlum tu illic es;* and I find Thee in the bottom of the deepest valleys, in sanctuaries unknown to the world ; whether I go to the east or to the west, whether I cross the seas, I find Thee always, O Sacrament, everywhere diffused, and it is Thou who leadest me and sustainest me by the virtue which emanates from Thy presence and Thy reception —*si descendero in infernum ades, si sumpsero pennas diluculo et habitavero in extremis maris, etenim illuc manus tua deducet me, et tenebit me dextera tua."*

Adore the omnipresence of God which renders Him present everywhere in order to see all things, to govern all things, to sustain all things, and to judge all things. See how well the Eucharist represents Him ; through it as through the omnipresence, we may say with Saint Gregory that the Lord is above all things, guiding all things, beneath all things in order to sustain all things, surrounding all things to maintain all things in unity ; penetrating all things in order to vivify all things—*sursum regens, deorsum continens, extra circumdans et intra penetrans.* Above all things, the principle of life in the Church, the source whence all the other sacraments are derived ; below all things, bearing, sustaining the world, the Church, souls, foundation of all that is, root of all that grows ; around all, enveloping our souls with its power, with its protection, maintaining the Church in unity, and preserving it from schisms, and it is still it which penetrates into souls by means of its virtue, its substance, its very being, to make them live a supernatural life, His own life, which is justice and holiness.

Adore in this universal diffusion of the Eucharist the actual and effective royalty of Our Lord. His Father said to Him, "I will give Thee the nations to rule over —*dabo tibi possessionem tuam terminos terræ;* Our Lord, in diffusing Himself, seems to traverse the provinces of His empire everywhere to collect the adorations, the praises, the homage which is due to Him; He desires that everywhere, at one and the same time, knees should bend and hearts bow down before Him.

This quasi-infinity of the Eucharist is full of sublime mysteries; adore them, and transporting yourself in spirit in all places where there is manifested the presence of love, of goodness, of life, of omnipotence of the God in the Eucharist, adore Him, praise Him, bless Him with the angels who hasten around Him and follow Him everywhere.

II. THANKSGIVING.

Cum dilexisset, in finem dilexit (John xiii.).
"Having loved, He loved to the end."

But wherefore this presence of Jesus in the sacrament? Through love, through goodness, through friendship for man.

Presence is necessary to friendship. Absence is the death of it—*nil tam proprium est amicitiæ quam convivere amico.* Now, we are all His friends; His love has so willed it and has given us the name; and from that time forward He desires to come to all and each one of us, as near as He can!

Ruth said to Naomi, who was obliged to go back to

her own land, "*Quo perrexeris, pergam!*" And Our Lord says to every Christian, "Wherever thou shalt go I will go that I may not be separated from thee! In deserts and in solitary places, on the mountains, in populous towns, and in unknown villages, everywhere! Thy country shall be My country, and thy people My people!"

Ah, what blessings flow from this universal presence!

Even as the presence of the Ark of the Covenant was strength, the security, victory, honor, and benediction for all the places where it resided, so is the Eucharist. Through it we are rendered strong, and Satan is weakened, arrested, chained. Through it we are great; God is our co-citizen, the inhabitant of our towns, and our compatriot. Through it man, whoever he may be, always finds his God; has recourse to Him without difficulty, without fatigue. If it were necessary to one sole church which alone had the privilege of keeping Him, where should we be able to find men capable of such a sacrifice? But He is there, here, beside us, with us, O abundance of heavenly condescension!

In multiplying His presence He multiplies the graces which each Host brings with it; and each Host is worth the salvation of the world, and pays all the graces of which the world has need. There is the buckler extended over the whole earth and beneath which the nations are sheltered from the darts of Divine Justice irritated by the sins of the world. Ah, how beautiful, covered by its white harvest of consecrated Hosts, is our poor earth, in spite of its ugliness; fruitful, in spite of its sterility; holy, in spite of its crimes; beloved by God, in spite of the hatred with which it repays His love! *Confiteantur tibi Domine populi omnes, terra dedit fructum suum!*

III. Propitiation.

Medius vestrum stetit quem vos nescitis (John i. 26).
"There hath stood one in the midst of you whom you know not."

Numquid solitudo factus sum Israeli ! (Jer. ii. 31).
"Am I become a wilderness to Israel ?"

Alas ! Our Lord can never testify His great love for us without costing Him great sacrifices and great humiliations. First of all, by multiplying His presence He exposes Himself to having in many poor places dwellings unworthy of Him. But in order to be with His children wherever they are, He forgets the splendor due to Him and contents Himself with anything !

If it were only poverty that was the result of the diffusion of His sacrament ! But there is more than this—we accustom ourselves to see Him everywhere. The excess of the favor becomes an occasion of humiliation for Him, and attention is no longer paid to His presence. If it were less diffused we should go to Him, carrying His condescension to its utmost limits, we abuse it for the purpose of disowning Him. Behold Him in all the churches alone day and night ; no one enters them. Elsewhere on seeing His churches they are blasphemed ; here, again, crowds pass before His dwelling and not even cast a glance upon Him ! He is there, nevertheless, at the centre and in the heart of the city ; His presence shows itself by the appearance, the splendor, the majesty of His dwelling, but all is asleep, and it is as though He were not there !

And to what humiliating neighborhood is not Our Lord sometimes subjected ! What places of unjust dealing, what dishonorable houses are established beside

Him! And those who frequent them disturb by the sound of their orgies the peace of His dwelling. Ah! let your souls be touched by all these things, pity and compassionate the indifference shown to the dwellings of Jesus and be afflicted by the sacrilegious affronts which are inflicted upon Him.

Above all console this divine Friend, who, placing Himself thus within our reach, is so little known, so little visited, so little honored. Unknown in the midst of His own! It is an incomprehensible phenomenon sufficient to cast us into a state of stupor. He is here, there, everywhere, beneath our eyes, beneath our feet, and we do not know how to find Him! We make a pretext of fatigue, of want of leisure for not visiting Him, in spite of His having made so many advances for the purpose of coming to us!

Specially ask pardon for all the visits you have neglected to make to Him when you might have done so, for all the impulses of false shame which have prevented you from rendering a public homage to His presence by a sign of religion when you have passed before His dwellings. Lastly, have pity on Jesus isolated, lost, unknown in certain heretic, infidel, or impious countries. He is there nevertheless! He sighs there; send your heart to His feet in order to console Him!

IV. Prayer.

Domine, sequar te quocumque ieris (Matt. viii. 19).
"Master, I will follow Thee whithersoever Thou shalt go."

I ask of Thee, O divine unknown One, to make Thyself to be known, loved, and served by all those in the midst of whom Thou hast so long, so humbly, so lovingly dwelt!

I beg Thee to diffuse Thyself still more ; and I specially entreat Thee for missionaries that they may build every day for Thee new sanctuaries and ceaselessly conquer for Thee fresh kingdoms !

As for me, O Jesus, I beg of Thee to make me respond to the love which diffuses Thee for my sake and brings Thee near to me, by a love which attaches me to Thee, makes me seek Thy presence and find my happiness in living always with Thee, beside Thee, under the blessed ray of Thy Host—*ut inhabitem in domo Domini omnibus diebus vitæ meæ !*

And, above all, O Jesus, in the same way that by Thy sacrament Thou art with me everywhere, grant me to be with Thee always, to carry Thee with me everywhere, by my fidelity ; to be present to Thee even when I have left Thy tabernacles, to see Thee still, to live beneath Thy eyes, and to remain united with Thee everywhere, in solitary labor, in my family relations ; in my public employments, in my social intercourse, in my worldly affairs ; with Thee everywhere !

May nothing ever separate me from Thee, may I always reach out to Thee through desire and through love ; and may there never be an hour in my life which is not enlightened, rendered fruitful, and sanctified by the sun of Thy presence in the sacrament !

The Perpetuity of the Eucharist.

ALWAYS!

I. Adoration.

Adore Jesus instituting the Eucharist, to endure till the end of the world, and saying those memorable words: "*Behold I am with you all days, even to the consummation of the world.*" The words of the Saviour are realized: behold the Eucharist has lasted nineteen centuries, and it will endure till the evening of the last day of the world to fortify the last of the elect fighting against Antichrist.

This perpetuity of the Eucharist is full of marvels; it must be studied and adored; it is a sublime manifestation of the Eternal who hides Himself beneath the feeble species of the sacrament.

The Eucharist is eternal. This Host was consecrated this morning, it has just been born upon the altar, in the midst of the profound silence of the mysteries; it is about to be consumed by the priest; it will have lasted only a moment; in spite of that it is the Eternal! He whom one single word has made to appear, created the worlds; He possessed the plenitude of life before anything existed; He whose sacramental life is about to be extinguished in so unperceived a manner, is the

Master of life and of death. He alone gives life; alone He maintains it in all that is, and all that dies is judged by Him. Holy Eucharist, I adore Thee; Thou art He who was, who is, and who shall be forever!

The perpetuity of the Eucharist is a mirror in which is reflected the ineffable properties of the divine eternity. Eternity is the total and simultaneous possession of an interminable life, it is the duration, the immutability, the possession always the same of a perfect life. Now, behold Thou hast existed for more than nineteen centuries, and Thou wilt exist to the end, O Sacrament of life; Thou dost possess the divine life of Christ and His mortal life and His life of glory; and in this plenitude Thou art always young, always fruitful, always omnipotent! All these long centuries, Thy journeys over the world, these interminable expectations, persecutions, sacrileges, evil treatment, nothing has been able to take away Thy eucharistic life; Thou hast resisted all things! Generations have passed away, empires have been destroyed, and in that torrent, which once let loose, carries away everything and is stopped by nothing, Thou dost remain like an indestructible rock, affirming the eternity of Him whom Thou dost contain, His immutability, His perfect life, down to the day when the elect will know it by experience in the kingdom of endless delights!

Let us adore, then, the eternity of God, let us adore the omnipotence and the infinite love which have created and which maintain the perpetuity of the Real Presence; there is as much power displayed in each of the moments of the duration of the Eucharist as in its institution itself.

O sublime spectacle! This Host which a breath of air would cast to the ground, which a drop of water would dissolve, which an insect could devour, it is it which bears the world and gives it life! It is for it that Jesus founded the Church, the Papacy, the priesthood, and the sacraments; for it that idols have been thrown down, peoples made Christian, and the face of the earth renewed; adore, praise, sing; it is the living God, it is the Eternal—*Ipse est enim Deus vivens et œternus!* (Dan. vi. 26.)

II. THANKSGIVING.

If the perpetuity of the Eucharist shows forth the eternity of God and His power, it is a still more striking proof of His love, of His goodness, of His condescension towards us. This perpetuity is the source of all blessing, of all grace, of all succor for the Church and for souls.

If Jesus had only instituted the Eucharist for the apostles, where would their successors have been enkindled with the sacred fire of the apostolate? where would martyrs have found strength to resist torments? where would doctors have gone for enlightenment? how would the Church have lived? where would she have derived for the barbarians who delivered themselves up to her to be formed, as well as for the pagan empire which she was destined to transfigure, the aliment of supernatural virtues which has made nations Christian and has formed saints and has produced civilization?

If Jesus had not perpetuated Himself in the Eucharist, who is there who would still know Him? Who would love Him? Who would love Him enough, I say, to prefer Him to all things, to sacrifice everything to Him to the point of being attached to Him alone and to make of His service and of His good pleasure the passion of a life and the satisfaction of the most ardent ambitions? Is not absence the death of love? If Jesus had not perpetuated Himself in the Eucharist, the virtue, the examples, the merits, the fruits, and the efficacies of the Incarnation and of all its mysteries, of the passion and of all its sufferings, what would be their action, their influence over the world at the present moment? Forgetfulness would have enveloped and extinguished all; the ingratitude of men would have dried up the source of the goodness of God; Satan, for a moment dethroned, would have resumed his sway; the scandals of paganism would have forever engulfed souls and society in their mire.

If Jesus were not to remain upon this altar of perpetual prayer where He offers day and night His sacrifice of annihilation, when He shows to His Father the wounds in His members, and His Heart consumed with love, with sighs, and with desires—if this mediation was not of a continuity which knows no weariness, nor sleep, nor distraction, and which is active, ardent, obstinate as the love itself, what scourges would there not be inflicted upon the world by our sins renewed without ceasing, our monstrous ingratitude, the blasphemies and apostasies of baptized Christians and of redeemed nations?

Lastly, if Jesus were not to remain in the Eucharist, how should we communicate with God? Where would be the sensible presence of the Creator of which creatures stand in such need? The earth without the neighborhood and the presence of God would be exile, death, hell.

The Incarnation continued, the Redemption applied, the world saved, the divine scourges turned aside, the Church sustained, God, the good, the true, kept here below as the patrimony of the children of the Church—such, then, are the blessings of the perpetuity of the Eucharist for the world: give thanks, be grateful, for nothing of all this was due to us; love alone has done all, given all.

And if, to the benefits of the perpetuity for the Church in general, you add the innumerable benefits you derive from it for yourself, into what thanksgivings will you not burst forth?

Jesus has remained since the Last Supper, awaiting you in the thrice blessed meeting of your First Communion; nineteen centuries of waiting, of sacrifices, and of humiliation have not seemed too long to His love in order to keep for you, and at last to bring you, joy which has no equal!

He still remains and follows you to bless the labor of the day, He remains with you in the evening to repair the defects in it and to consecrate its fruits, and when the most persevering in prayer retire, when you go and take your rest He recommences His nightly watch, for His love knows no repose and His eyes never close over you.

He will remain thus that you may always and at every moment find Him; He will never make you wait; never will He send you away; and you could not give Him a greater pleasure than to be occupied largely with Him, to confide to Him all your troubles, and to have nothing hidden from Him. He will remain till your last day, that He may console it and illuminate it with hope; and when you quit this world, leaving your nearest and dearest orphans or afflicted, He will remain, His day is never over, His task never accomplished, He has said so, "until the consummation of the world."

He will remain even when you do not remain, during your forgetfulness, your coldness, your long infidelities, your apostasies. He remains to prepare your return by praying for you, and to receive you, to pardon you, and to press you to His Heart, when, filled with remorse, with repentance and weariness, you return, a prodigal child, to knock at the door of the paternal mansion.

He remains because it is the characteristic of love to be patient, constant, indefatigable, and never to die!

Read over again the golden pages of your life in which the Eucharist has written down its innumerable benefits, and it will be with tears that you will then thank the loving Saviour for the inexpressible gift of His Heart!

III. Propitiation.

But at the price of what sacrifices does Jesus buy the right of remaining always with us in the sacrament, the perpetuity of which is so beautiful and so good?

The perpetuity exposes Him primarily to isolation, to that sorrowful solitude in which we see Him in so many churches. If He only came for a few hours every day, or for a single day every year, we might then surround Him and not leave Him for a moment; but He wills to remain always, in spite of being left to come after the necessities of life, daily labor, household occupations, and even after legitimate pleasures; for a God, surrounded in heaven by a court which never ceases praising Him, what an incomprehensible sacrifice!

If the duties of our state or those imposed by charity were alone preferred to Him, He has wished it beforehand and would bear it easily. But, alas! the very perpetuity of His presence occasions Him to be forgotten, to be forsaken, and to cause us to prefer to Him all that attracts and seduces by its novelty—pleasures, vain conversations, worldly pastimes; we love better to spend our time in doing nothing than in going to spend a few moments with the most tender of friends who gives us all His time.

There are those, however, whose vocation it is to keep Him company and to honor His perpetual presence by their frequent prayers, but what negligence do even they show in their relations with Our Lord! The visit is suppressed on the slightest pretext, or at any rate it is abridged; all that presents itself in concurrence with this capital duty has the upper hand; and, in a word, it is the presence of Our Lord which is disdained!

And, lastly, those who come, those who consecrate almost all the time that is requisite in order to honor so august a presence, how do they employ it? Does it not often seem to them to be long and wearisome? Long, when He, the Creator, the Lord of lords, is always there? wearisome, when the God of beatitude finds His delights in being with the children of men?

Let us weep, then, and make reparation for this crime of absence, so sensible to the always-present Heart of Jesus. Let us repair by our presence, by multiplying our visits, by prolonging them, by feeling, what is indeed true, that "an hour spent in His temple is worth more than a century in a palace of sinners"! But what reparations would be capable of satisfying for the irreverences, the outrages, the sacrileges of which His perpetual presence is the object?

What numberless churches badly kept! What tabernacles where His presence is not even made known by the humble light of the sacred lamp! How many Christians pass whole months and years without going a single time to honor Him who loved them even to Calvary, and who cannot resolve to forget them! How many wretched creatures who utter horrible blasphemies at the mere sight of the dwelling of Jesus! How He is maltreated by the sacrilegious who profit by the condescension with which even in the obscurity and the silence of night He wills to remain defenceless in our churches to watch over His children who sleep and to keep from them infernal prowlers !

In spite of all this Jesus has sworn from the beginning that He will always remain, and He keeps the word of His love. Even as Judas did not prevent Him from beginning, so the traitors of all ages will not hinder Him from continuing ; it is more than we can understand ! But ought not reparation, love, fidelity to respond to so much love ? Ah, do not let us remain insensible to the words which escape day and night from all the tabernacles, like the sigh of the adorable forsaken Master, " I have stretched out My hands all day long to a people who deny and reject Me."

IV. Supplication.

" *Mane nobiscum, Domine, quoniam advesperascit—* Master, remain with us, for it is growing late !"

Remain in this world, O Jesus, remain in it always, in spite of its coldness, its indifference and its crimes, for without Thy perpetual presence it would be nothing but a field of carnage, a sink of vices, a land where Satan and sin would reign uncontested masters ; remain to purify it, oppose Thy purity to its stains, Thy prayers to its blasphemies, Thy adorations to its idolatries !

Remain with the Church, O Jesus, to vivify her in her soul, to sustain her in her combats, to conduct her in her paths, to console her in her defeats ; remain at the present day more than ever, for never was there an hour more difficult, and Thou art her Husband, her Spouse, and her King !

Remain with her Vicar and assist him in all his enterprises ; console him for the ingratitude of his rebellious children; remain and sustain his old age, O Host of life and of salvation !

Remain with Thy priests, Thy monks, and Thy nuns, and inspire them with the desire, the need, the passion of Thy presence in the sacrament! May they find their happiness in keeping near Thee, may they lovingly surround Thee, and may they comprehend that it is their primary mission and the most powerful of apostolates !

Make Thyself to be known by those who are ignorant of Thee, O beneficent presence of Jesus! make them feel their need of Thee, and after having found in Thee the succor or the consolation which they felt, may they attach themselves to Thee forever !

Remain with me, O Jesus, to-day, always! Never deprive me of Thy presence—far from Thee, whither should I go, without Thee what would become of me ?

I ask of Thee grace, and I make the resolution to apply myself very seriously to the great duty of honoring Thy presence with visits and by adoration; to prepare myself for this audience, not without absolute necessity to cut it short by a single moment; to esteem it at its right value; to employ it with the fidelity, the pious eagerness of love and of gratitude !

O Jesus, remain !

Thou art always here below in Thy sacrament !

Thou art in heaven in Thy glory !

The Universality of the Eucharist.

TO ALL!

I. Adoration.

" Take and eat ye all of it!"
" Drink ye all of it!"

Adore Our Lord in the universal gift which He makes of His Eucharist, and listen with joy, love, admiration, and in the silence of the most profound adoration, the liberal, generous, magnificent, royal, and truly divine words of Jesus, "Take and eat ye all of it"! *Omnes*, all! All, to-day! All, to-morrow, and throughout all ages—All!

Adore the infinite knowledge of Jesus, His wholly divine foresight. He embraces in His fatherly glance all those of all times and of all nations who, till the end, shall be born of His blood, and shall enter into His family, and He prepares for all the bread which alone can nourish their supernatural life and satisfy their divine appetites.

Adore the omnipotence of Jesus, who is about to deposit in the priesthood of His apostles and of their successors the power of reproducing His great action, and of endlessly diffusing the sacrament of His body multiplied beyond all measure. Adore the ardor, the energy, the exuberance of His love which really drags Him beyond the limits of all that is possible and credible, and which makes the flood of His Eucharist with which He wills to cover the world and to envelop souls never cease to pour forth from His Heart and His hands.

Adore, admire, praise, bless, be silent—love, love !

Then behold with what generous fidelity, with what magnificent plenitude He realizes before your eyes the gift of the Eucharist.

He gives it to all ; as many as they are, so many is He ! In however great numbers they may come, there are always more Hosts than Christians. They are counted by hundreds, they are counted by thousands ; the ciboriums are filled, and when all the guests have feasted on the bread of the true life there remains some still for those who are late in coming, for the infirm, for unforeseen needs, and the Church, that beautiful mother, keeps always in the granaries of her tabernacles inexhaustible provisions of wheat for the people she has to feed.

What power ! At the service of what bounty ! To multiply to such a point the most precious of all things, the most wonderful of miracles, the most beautiful masterpiece of the divine hand, which is worth all heaven, and which is God Himself !

In all the churches throughout the Catholic world there is a ciborium ; put into each ciborium twenty Hosts ; then count, if you can, the number of these adorable Hosts, cast before the footsteps of Christians by the love and the power of a heart devoured by the need to give itself in order to make itself loved ! Jesus, O Jesus ! hast Thou set more stars in the heavens than Thou hast placed Hosts in our churches ? Are there more leaves in our thick forests, and more grains of sand on the shores of the ocean ?

It has been well said of Thee by the inspired prophet, "Thou openest Thy hand and Thou fillest all Thy children with this consecrated bread, this bread of blessing;" and once open, Thy hand is never again closed; it is a deep source, a boundless sea, a shoreless ocean, the ocean of the Eucharist.

In giving Himself to all Jesus gives Himself fully to each, and the gift of the one does not injure the plenitude of the gift made to the other. It is the triumph of His goodness.

Even as the sun, while diffusing everywhere the same light and the same heat, produces at the same time a thousand different effects, animates life in sentient beings, makes the vegetable world grow, renders the earth fruitful, and dries up bad waters, makes the garden blossom and the orchard ripen, giving to each kind of fruit its flavor, to each flower its splendor and its perfume, so does the goodness of Jesus in the universal gift of the Eucharist.

The holy table is surrounded by Christians of all ages, of all conditions, having all of them divers and special needs. The same Host given to all corresponds to the desires, to the special needs of each; it is it which the sun of souls renders fertile and ripens all kinds of fruit; it is it which makes all the flowers in the garden of the Church blossom and beautifully colored; the Christian young man with noble ardors, the virgin the rival of angels, the man faithful to God in the labors of life; the Christian woman, the mother of souls still more than of bodies, old age resigned and full of hopes. It is it which gives to the priest his authority, to the religious the strength of voluntary mortification, to the missionary the heroism of a sublime devotedness. And while giving itself with royal liberality and an inestimable generosity, it also acts indefatigably, as perseveringly, as generously, lovingly, in a word, loving "to the end," and as far as the extreme limits of a love which does not seem to be even aware of it !

O love, O treasure, O proof of love ! Jesus given, Jesus who thus grants the whole of Thyself in the sacrament, I love Thee ; ah ! let me die now if I must live without loving Thee.

II. THANKSGIVING.

" Take and eat ye all ! *Omnes !*"

In this universal and magnificent gift see what an important share falls to you personally, in order that you may create in your breast a burning furnace of gratitude.

It required four thousand years to prepare the supreme gift of God for the world, and, behold, this gift is renewed every day for you in the communion, without formality, without pomp, almost without being announced ; nevertheless is it not the same Word who comes with as much power as love ? Well, count how many times Jesus has performed this incarnation of love in the communion for you !

First, on the day of your First Communion, do you remember the sweetness of this first gift, of its liberalities, of its royal munificence, of its tender love ? Since that count the communions of your youth and those which perhaps you make every day now. What ! every day Jesus renews for you, for you alone, the supreme gift, prepared by the waiting expectations of ages, the desires of all the patriarchs, the purity and the humility of Mary, and more even than that, prepared and given for the first time at the Last Supper by the love of the

Word Incarnate, and come as far as you at the price of His Passion and of His death?

Ah! "thanks! gratitude! love! for the inexpressible gift of Jesus!"

And see with what perseverance He has always given Himself to you! Always equally prompt, always equally eager, always equally good, always kind, always joyous; you have received Him during so many years; you have very often received Him with a tepid heart already taken up with worldly cares, or occupied with other loves, perhaps with a guilty heart; you have disdained Him for long, forgetful of His love, deaf to His solicitations; in spite of all does He not return to you with a love as pure, as ardent, as tender as on the first day?

See the operations of grace, the magnificent blossomings, the numberless fructifications which this gift has performed in you! In former years, a pure and refreshing balm, it moderated the ardor of your fiery passions; at the present day it sustains you in your labors and reanimates your weakened courage; at one time it was for your humility, at another time purity; at one time meekness, at another time firmness and energy; in your sorrows it was consolation to you, in your trials, hope, and the reanimation of you in your discouragements—in a word, in all suffering, in all grief, patience, resignation, and abandonment.

There is nothing good, nothing desirable, which you have not found in this bread of love if you have sought for it there; so that the same gift, so often repeated, multiplied itself over and over again to infinitude, by varying and transforming itself according to your daily needs.

It is the moment in which to give blessing and thanks in the effusion of your gratitude to the love which has given it to you; recall everything carefully to your remembrance, do not be afraid of dwelling too long upon each one of His marvellous bounties. Forget nothing! Everything has its price, and if you had communicated only one single time your gratitude ought to be eternal! *Benedic anima mea Domino et noli oblivisci omnes retributiones ejus!*

III. PROPITIATION.

"Take and eat ye all of it! *Omnes!*" Let your soul offer itself to a love of compassion towards Jesus, for His gift is not understood. His goodness seems to have carried Him too far, and the desire to prove His love to you at any price, to have blinded Him in respect to the interests of His honor and of His own glory.

In giving Himself to all with such prodigality, our Lord exposes Himself to be treated as a thing that is common and valueless, to be neglected, counted as little and despised, and even by those who are Christians, by those who receive Him and love Him in a certain manner.

The manna of the desert had excited nausea in the Israelites precisely on account of its extreme abundance. In the same way the Eucharist becomes to us a tasteless bread, a nourishment which has no savor, because it is offered to us every day and we find it without any trouble. Is not the great danger of frequent communion, tepid communion, with preparations made from routine and thanksgivings devoid of love?

Examine yourself upon this point and see what dispositions you bring to the communion.

How long a time, what methods, do you employ for the preparation and the thanksgiving? How do you behave at them?

Alas, alas! must Our Lord count us among the children whom He has nourished and elevated to a sublime honor and who have despised Him!

The second peril of dishonor to which this gift is exposed by being lavished so easily by the goodness of Jesus, is of falling into sacrilegious hands.

What, divine Master, Love too generous and too credulous, Thou wishest to give Thyself to all? To all without exception? To all without a preliminary examination and without an authoritative public permission? Even to sinners? Even to traitors? Even to hypocrites? Even to the Judases of the sacerdotal college?

Yes, to all, and even to Judas, and to all those who shall perpetuate his odious personality, I will give Myself without resistance, without any possible defence, without inflicting on them the slightest external shame; I will spare their honor, I will even serve to give them a reputation for piety; to all! I will to be delivered up to all! They will doubtless eat their own condemnation; it would be better for them not to have been born than to commit so black a sacrilege; nevertheless, if they come, I will allow Myself to be eaten; I prefer to be maltreated by some, leaving to all the opportunity of coming freely and thus giving a proof of how far My love goes, than to place barriers before the sacrilegious which might be also a hindrance to the timidity of the good. To all!

Oh, too good Master, dost Thou think of the terrible consequences of this promise which Thy love imposes on Thee? Dost Thou not behold these multitudes of heretics and schismatics? To all!

And these bad priests, usurious, indecent, rebellious to their bishops, who usurp the holy functions and ascend the altar? To all!

And at Easter the crowds who wish to keep up an appearance of Christianity without practising its august duties, and who come to receive you without renouncing their evil habits, without abjuring former hatreds, without making necessary restitutions, after confessions made without contrition as well as without firm resolutions, and by imposing a truce of a few days on their daily faults? To all!

Thou art not horrified, then, O Jesus, at passing through all these hands, at being subjected to all this unworthy treatment, and at facing all these ignominies?

Ah, yes! My heart is steeped in bitterness; the sight of it all makes Me shudder; such a chalice as this cannot be drunk without casting Me into mortal agony. Nevertheless I will give Myself to all, in order that the good who are themselves weak and tottering may dare to come to Me without fear; in order that the bad may end in allowing themselves to be conquered by so much love!

But I expect My friends to console Me, to make reparation for Me, to stand in the place of My enemies near Me, and to honor My gift which they despise! Oh, ye at least, ye who are My friends, have pity on Me and "receive My Eucharist in remembrance of Me"!

IV. SUPPLICATION.

"Take and eat ye all of it! *Omnes!*"

In giving Thyself thus to us, O Jesus, Thou dost testify with an undeniable evidence the desire which Thou hast to come into Thy creatures, to live in them, and to be to them all graces, all succor, all good. There is a need in Thy heart which Thy love renders more and more imperious, a hunger which is ceaselessly renewed.

Thou desirest with a desire as burning as Thy love itself, "to eat this Pasch with us." And Thou callest us, Thou entreatest us, Thou makest us to be sought, Thou conjurest, Thou dost even threaten—"Ah, take and eat ye all of this"!

Well, I will answer Thy appeal, satisfy Thy hunger, while entreating Thee by Thy own merits, by Thy Heart, and by all the love with which it burns for men, to touch and to gain all those who obstinately refuse Thy adorable gift, and into whom Thou wouldst be so happy to come for their happiness, for their salvation, for the peace of their heart, and the consolation of their life.

Jesus, Gift of God, make Thyself known to infidels and to heretics, to the indifferent or incredulous masses of Catholic nations! Bring them back; cast them on their knees, conquered and subjugated, around Thy holy table!

Make all at least approach it at Easter, and let them not find the death of their soul at the very moment in which Thou dost offer them the gift of life!

Jesus, oh, I ask it of Thee by Thy holiness and by Thy mercy, that all who receive Thee should do so with faith, with piety, with love, the conscience purified from all heinous sin, the heart disengaged from all guilty ties, with a sincere will to remain faithful to Thee!

Touch and convert the sacrilegious who prepare themselves to betray Thee, or make them depart, I beg of Thee, through terror of Thy justice, so that they may not lay upon Thy most holy person their impious hands!

And as for me, since Thou willest to give Thyself to me so often, to be my daily bread, and the support of my daily labor, since Thou willest to penetrate into my life, to become an integral portion of it, to be the soul, the moving power, and the indispensable element of it, since Thou willest to be everything to me, to share all my labors, to bear the half of all my crosses, and to join with me in all my joys—well, then, I promise Thee, and I earnestly ask of Thee grace to be faithful to my promise ; I will never voluntarily miss a single one of the communions which Thou dost permit me by the authority of Thy ministers !

I will purify myself more and more from sin, I will detach myself more and more every day from the servitude of the world, from the snares of my self-love, and I will make constant efforts after a sincerely Christian life, that I may merit to receive Thee worthily every day, and to profit by the graces contained in Thy sacrament.

And Thou wilt be all to me ; yes, all ! In order to avoid sin, I will receive Thee !

To correct my defects, I will receive Thee !

To bear my troubles, I will receive Thee !

To be charitable and devout, I will receive Thee !

And my prayer of every moment, that which I desire to make Thee in my heart and by my works, even when my lips are mute, is Thine, O Jesus, that which Thou hast taught me, and which includes all—" Give me, oh, give me my daily bread !" the bread of life, the bread of strength, the bread of honor, the bread of truth, the bread of love, the bread of immortality ; give me Thy Gift, to-day and always, here below in the Eucharist, in heaven in glory !

STANDARD CATHOLIC BOOKS

PUBLISHED BY

BENZIGER BROTHERS,

CINCINNATI:	NEW YORK:	CHICAGO:
343 Main St.	36 & 38 BARCLAY ST.	178 Monroe St.

ABANDONMENT; or, Absolute Surrender of Self to Divine Providence. By Rev. J. P. CAUSSADE, S.J. 32mo, *net*, 0 40

ALTAR BOY'S MANUAL, LITTLE. Illustrated. 32mo, 0 25

ANALYSIS OF THE GOSPELS of the Sundays of the Year. By Rev. L. A. LAMBERT, LL.D. 12mo, *net*, 1 25

ART OF PROFITING BY OUR FAULTS, according to St. Francis de Sales. By Rev. J. TISSOT. 32mo, *net*, 0 40

BIBLE, THE HOLY. With Annotations, References, and an Historical and Chronological Index. 12mo, cloth, 1 25

BIRTHDAY SOUVENIR, OR DIARY. With a Subject of Meditation for Every Day. By Mrs. A. E. BUCHANAN. 32mo, 0 50

BLESSED ONES OF 1888. 16mo, illustrated, 0 50

BLIND FRIEND OF THE POOR: Reminiscences of the Life and Works of Mgr. DE SEGUR. 16mo, 0 50

BLISSYLVANIA POST-OFFICE, THE. By MARION AMES TAGGART. 16mo, 0 50

BONE RULES; or, Skeleton of English Grammar. By Rev. J. B. Tabb. 16mo, *net*, 0 35

BOYS' AND GIRLS' MISSION BOOK. By the Redemptorist Fathers. 48mo, 0 35

BOYS' AND GIRLS' ANNUAL. 0 05

BROWNSON, ORESTES A., Literary, Scientific, and Political Views of. Selected from his works. 12mo, *net*, 1 25

BUGG, LELIA HARDIN. Correct Thing for Catholics. 16mo, 0 75

——— A Lady. Manners and Social Usages. 16mo, 1 00

BY BRANSCOME RIVER. By M. A. Taggart. 16mo, 0 50

CANTATA CATHOLICA. Containing a large collection of Masses, etc. HELLEBUSCH. Oblong 4to, *net*, 2 00

CATECHISM OF FAMILIAR THINGS. Their History and the Events which led to their Discovery. 12mo, illustrated, 1 00

CATHOLIC BELIEF; or, a Short and Simple Exposition of Catholic Doctrine. By the Very Rev. JOSEPH FAÀ DI BRUNO, D.D. 200th Thousand. 16mo.
  Paper, 0.25; 25 copies, 4.25; 50 copies, 7.50; 100 copies, 12 50
  Cloth, 0.50; 25 copies, 8.50; 50 copies, 15.00; 100 copies, 25 00
  "The amount of good accomplished by it can never be told."—*Catholic Union and Times.*

1

CATHOLIC CEREMONIES and Explanation of the Ecclesiastical Year. By the Abbé DURAND. With 96 illustrations. 24mo.
Paper, 0.25; 25 cop., 4.25; 50 cop., 7.50; 100 cop., 12 50
Cloth, 0.50; 25 cop., 8.50; 50 cop., 15.00; 100 cop., 25 00
A practical, handy volume for the people at a low price. It has been highly recommended by Cardinals, Archbishops, and Bishops.

CATHOLIC FAMILY LIBRARY. Composed of "The Christian Father," "The Christian Mother," "Sure Way to a Happy Marriage," "Instructions on the Commandments and Sacraments," and "Stories for First Communicants." 5 volumes in box, 2 00

CATHOLIC HOME ANNUAL. 0 25

CATHOLIC HOME LIBRARY. 10 volumes. 12mo, each, 0 45
Per Set, 3 00

CATHOLIC WORSHIP. The Sacraments, Ceremonies, and Festivals of the Church Explained. BRENNAN. Paper, 0.15; per 100, 9.00. Cloth, 0.25; per 100, 15 00

CATHOLIC YOUNG MAN OF THE PRESENT DAY. By Right Rev. AUGUSTINE EGGER, D.D. 32mo, cloth, 0.25; per 100, 15 00

CHARITY THE ORIGIN OF EVERY BLESSING. 16mo, 0 75

CHILD OF MARY. A complete Prayer-Book for Children of Mary. 32mo, 0 60

CHRIST IN TYPE AND PROPHECY. By Rev. A. J. MAAS, S.J. 2 vols., 12mo, *net*, 4 00

CHRISTIAN ANTHROPOLOGY. By Rev. J. THEIN. 8vo, *net*, 2 50

CHRISTIAN FATHER, THE: What he Should be, and What he Should Do. Paper, 0.25; per 100, 12.50. Cloth, 0.35; per 100, 21 00

CHRISTIAN MOTHER, THE: the Education of her Children and her Prayer. Paper, 0.25; per 100, 12.50. Cloth, 0.35; per 100, 21 00

CIRCUS-RIDER'S DAUGHTER, THE. A novel. By F. v. BRACKEL. 12mo, 1 25

CLARKE, REV. RICHARD F., S.J. The Devout Year. Short Meditations. 24mo, *net*, 0 60

COBBETT, W. History of the Protestant Reformation. New Edition with Notes and Preface, by Very Rev. F. A. GASQUET, D.D., O.S.B., 12mo, cloth, *net*, 0 50

COMEDY OF ENGLISH PROTESTANTISM, THE. Edited by A. F. MARSHALL, B.A. Oxon. 12mo, *net*, 0 50

COMPENDIUM SACRAE LITURGIAE Juxta Ritum Romanum una cum Appendice De Jure Ecclesiastico Particulari in America Foederata Sept. vigente scripsit P. WAPELHORST, O.S.F. 8vo, *net*, 2 50

CONFESSIONAL, THE. By Right Rev. A. Roegel, D.D. Translated by Rev. Augustine Wirth, O.S.B. 12mo, *net*, 1 00

CONNOR D'ARCY'S STRUGGLES. A novel. By Mrs. W. M. BERTHOLDS. 12mo, 1 25

COUNSELS OF A CATHOLIC MOTHER to Her Daughter. 16mo, 0 50

CROWN OF MARY, THE. A Complete Manual of Devotion for Clients of the Blessed Virgin. 32mo, 0 60

CROWN OF THORNS, THE; or, The Little Breviary of the Holy Face. 32mo, 0 50

DATA OF MODERN ETHICS EXAMINED, THE. By Rev. JOHN J. MING, S.J. 12mo, *net*, 2 00

DE GOESBRIAND, RIGHT REV. L. Christ on the Altar. 4to, richly illustrated, gilt edges, 6 00
—— Jesus the Good Shepherd. 16mo, *net*, 0 75
—— The Labors of the Apostles. 12mo, *net*, 1 00

DEVOTIONS AND PRAYERS BY ST. ALPHONSUS. A Complete Prayer-Book. 16mo, 1 00

EGAN, MAURICE F. The Vocation of Edward Conway. A novel. 12mo, 1 25
—— Flower of the Flock, and Badgers of Belmont. 12mo, 1 00
—— How They Worked Their Way, and Other Stories, 1 00
—— The Boys in the Block. 24mo, leatherette, 0 25
—— A Gentleman. 16mo, 0 75

ENGLISH READER. By Rev. EDWARD CONNOLLY, S.J. 12mo, 1 25

EPISTLES AND GOSPELS. 32mo, 0 25

EUCHARISTIC CHRIST, THE. Reflections and Considerations on the Blessed Sacrament. By Rev. A. TESNIERE. 12mo, *net*, 1 00

EUCHARISTIC GEMS. A Thought about the Most Blessed Sacrament for Every Day. By Rev. L. C. COELENBIER. 16mo, 0 75

EXAMINATION OF CONSCIENCE for the use of Priests who are Making a Retreat. By GADUEL. 32mo, *net*, 0 30

EXPLANATION OF THE BALTIMORE CATECHISM of Christian Doctrine. By Rev. THOMAS L. KINKEAD. 12mo, *net*, 1 00

EXPLANATION OF THE COMMANDMENTS, ILLUSTRATED. By Rev. H. ROLFUS, D.D. With a Practice and Reflection on each Commandment, by Very Rev. F. GIRARDEY, C.SS.R. 16mo, 0 75

This is a very interesting and instructive explanation of the Commandments of God and of the Church, with numerous examples, anecdotes, Scripture passages, etc.

EXPLANATION OF THE GOSPELS, and Explanation of Catholic Worship. 24mo, illustrated.
Paper, 0.25; 25 copies, 4.25; 50 copies, 7.50; 100 copies, 12 50
Cloth, 0.50; 25 copies, 8 50; 50 copies, 15.00; 100 copies, 25 00

EXPLANATION OF THE MASS. By Father VON COCHEM. Preface by Bishop MAES. 12mo, 1 25

EXPLANATION OF THE OUR FATHER AND THE HAIL MARY. Adapted by Rev. RICHARD BRENNAN, LL.D. 16mo, 0 75

EXPLANATION OF THE SALVE REGINA. By St. ALPHONSUS LIGUORI. 16mo, 0 75

EXPLANATION OF THE PRAYERS AND CEREMONIES OF THE MASS, ILLUSTRATED. By Rev. I. D. LANSLOTS, O.S.B. With 22 full page illustrations. 12mo, 1 25
  Clearly explains the meaning of the altar, of its ornaments, of the vestments, of the prayers, and of the ceremonies performed by the celebrant and his ministers.

EXTREME UNCTION. Paper, 10 cents; per 100, 5 00
  The same in German at the same prices.

FABIOLA; or, The Church of the Catacombs. By CARDINAL WISEMAN. Illustrated Edition. 12mo, 1 25
  Edition de luxe, 6 00

FATAL DIAMONDS, THE. By ELEANOR C. DONNELLY. 24mo, fancy leatherette binding, 0 25

FINN, REV. FRANCIS J., S.J. Percy Wynn; or, Making a Boy of Him. 12mo, 0 85
—— Tom Playfair; or, Making a Start. 12mo, 0 85
—— Harry Dee; or, Working it Out. 12mo, 0 85
—— Claude Lightfoot; or, How the Problem was Solved. 12mo, 0 85
—— Ethelred Preston; or, The Adventures of a Newcomer. 12mo, 0 85
—— That Football Game, and What Came of It. 12mo, 0 85
—— Mostly Boys. 16mo, 0 85
—— My Strange Friend. 24mo, leatherette, 0 25

FIRST COMMUNICANT'S MANUAL. Small 32mo, 0 50

FIVE O'CLOCK STORIES; or, The Old Tales Told Again. 16mo, 0 75

FLOWERS OF THE PASSION. Thoughts of St. Paul of the Cross. By Rev. LOUIS TH. DE JÉSUS-AGONISANT. 32mo, 0 50

FOLLOWING OF CHRIST, THE. By THOMAS À KEMPIS.
  With reflections. Small 32mo, cloth, 0 50
  Without reflections. Small 32mo, cloth, 0 45
  Edition de luxe. Illustrated. From 1 50 up.

FRANCIS DE SALES, ST. Guide for Confession and Communion. Translated by Mrs. BENNETT-GLADSTONE. 32mo, 0 60
—— Maxims and Counsels for Every Day. 32mo, 0 50
—— New Year Greetings. 32mo, flexible cloth, 15 cents; per 100, 10 00

GENERAL PRINCIPLES OF THE RELIGIOUS LIFE. By Very Rev. BONIFACE F. VERHEYEN, O.S.B. 32mo, *net*, 0 30

GLORIES OF DIVINE GRACE. From the German of Dr. M. Jos. SCHEEBEN, by a BENEDICTINE MONK. 12mo, *net*, 1 50

GLORIES OF MARY. By St. Alphonsus. 2 vols. 12mo, *net*, 2 50

GOD KNOWABLE AND KNOWN. RONAYNE. 12mo, *net*, 1 25

GOFFINE'S DEVOUT INSTRUCTIONS. Illustrated Edition.
  Preface by His Eminence Cardinal GIBBONS. 8vo, cloth, 1.00; 10 copies, 7.50; 25 copies, 17.50; 50 copies, 33 50
  This is the best, the cheapest, and the most popular illustrated edition of Goffine's Instructions.

"GOLDEN SANDS," Books by the Author of:
 Golden Sands. Little Counsels for the Sanctification and Happiness of Daily Life. Third, Fourth, Fifth Series. 32mo, each, 0 60
 Book of the Professed. 32mo.
  Vol. I. ⎫
  Vol. II. ⎬ Each with a steel-plate Frontispiece. ⎧ *net*, 0 75
  Vol. III. ⎭   ⎨ *net*, 0 60
                         ⎩ *net*, 0 60
 Prayer. 32mo,   *net*, 0 40
 The Little Book of Superiors. 32mo,   *net*, 0 60
 Spiritual Direction. 32mo,   *net*, 0 60
 Little Month of May. 32mo, flexible cloth,   0 25
 Little Month of the Poor Souls. 32mo, flexible cloth, 0 25
 Hints on Letter-Writing. 16mo,   0 60

GROU, REV. J., S.J. The Characteristics of True Devotion. A new edition, by Rev. SAMUEL H. FRISBEE, S.J. 16mo, *net*, 0 75

——— The Interior of Jesus and Mary. Edited by Rev. SAMUEL H. FRISBEE, S.J. 16mo, 2 vols., *net*, 2 00

HANDBOOK FOR ALTAR SOCIETIES, and Guide for Sacristans and others having charge of the Altar and Sanctuary. 16mo. *net*, 0 75

HANDBOOK OF THE CHRISTIAN RELIGION. By Rev. W. WILMERS, S.J. From the German. Edited by Rev. JAMES CONWAY, S.J. 12mo, *net*, 1 50

HAPPY YEAR, A; or, The Year Sanctified by Meditating on the Maxims and Sayings of the Saints. By ABBÉ LASAUSSE. 12mo, *net*, 1 00

HEART, THE, OF ST. JANE FRANCES DE CHANTAL. Thoughts and Prayers. 32mo, *net*, 0 40

HEIR OF DREAMS, AN. By SALLIE MARGARET O'MALLEY. 16mo, 0 50

HELP FOR THE POOR SOULS IN PURGATORY. Sm. 32mo, 0 50

HIDDEN TREASURE; or, The Value and Excellence of the Holy Mass. By ST. LEONARD OF PORT-MAURICE. 32mo, 0 50

HISTORY OF THE CATHOLIC CHURCH. By Dr. H. BRUECK. 2 vols., 8vo, *net*, 3 00

HISTORY OF THE CATHOLIC CHURCH. Adapted by Rev. RICHARD BRENNAN, LL.D. With 90 Illustrations. 8vo, 1 50

HISTORY OF THE MASS and its Ceremonies in the Eastern and Western Church. By Rev. JOHN O'BRIEN, A.M. 12mo, *net*, 1 25

HOLY FACE OF JESUS, THE. A Series of Meditations on the Litany of the Holy Face. 32mo, 0 50

HOURS BEFORE THE ALTAR; or, Meditations on the Holy Eucharist. By Mgr. DE LA BOUILLERIE. 32mo, 0 50

HOW TO GET ON. By Rev. BERNARD FEENEY. 12mo, 1 00

HOW TO MAKE THE MISSION. By a Dominican Father. 16mo, paper, 10 cents; per 100, 5 00

HUNOLT'S SERMONS. *Complete Unabridged Edition.* Translated from the original German edition of Cologne, 1740, by the Rev. J. ALLEN, D.D. 12 vols., 8vo,   30 00
Vols. 1, 2. The Christian State of Life.
Vols. 3, 4. The Bad Christian.
Vols. 5, 6. The Penitent Christian.
Vols. 7, 8. The Good Christian.
Vols. 9, 10. The Christian's Last End.
Vols. 11, 12. The Christian's Model.

His Eminence Cardinal Gibbons, Archbishop of Baltimore: "... Contain a fund of solid doctrine, presented in a clear and forcible style. These sermons should find a place in the library of every priest. ..."

HUNOLT'S SHORT SERMONS. *Abridged Edition.* Arranged for all the Sundays of the year. 8vo, 5 vols.,   *net*, 10 00

IDOLS; or, The Secret of the Rue Chaussée d'Antin. A novel. By RAOUL DE NAVERY. 12mo,   1 25

ILLUSTRATED PRAYER-BOOK FOR CHILDREN. 32mo, 0 35

IMITATION OF THE BLESSED VIRGIN MARY. After the Model of the Imitation of Christ. Translated by Mrs. A. R. BENNETT-GLADSTONE. Small 32mo,   0 50
Edition de luxe, with fine illustrations. 32mo, from 1 50 up.

INSTRUCTIONS ON THE COMMANDMENTS and the Sacraments. By ST. LIGUORI. 32mo. Paper, 0.25; per 100, 12 50
Cloth, 0.35; per 100,   21 00

KONINGS, THEOLOGIA MORALIS. Novissimi Ecclesiæ Doctoris S. Alphonsi. Editio septima, auctior, et novis curis expolitior, curante HENRICO KUPER, C.SS.R. Two vols. in one, half morocco,   *net*, 4 00

——— Commentarium in Facultates Apostolicas. New, greatly enlarged edition. 12mo,   *net*, 2 25

——— General Confession Made Easy. 32mo, flex.,   0 15

LAMP OF THE SANCTUARY. A tale. Wiseman. 48mo, 0 25

LEGENDS AND STORIES OF THE HOLY CHILD JESUS from Many Lands. Collected by A. FOWLER LUTZ. 16mo, 0 75

LEPER QUEEN, THE. A Story of the Thirteenth Century. 16mo,   0 50

LETTERS OF ST. ALPHONSUS LIGUORI. Centenary Edition. 5 vols., 12mo. Each,   *net*, 1 25

LIBRARY OF THE RELIGIOUS LIFE. Composed of "Book of the Professed," by the author of "Golden Sands," 3 vols.; "Spiritual Direction," by the author of "Golden Sands"; and "Souvenir of the Novitiate." 5 vols., 32mo, in case,   3 25

LIFE AND ACTS OF LEO XIII. By Rev. JOSEPH E. KELLER, S.J. Fully and beautifully illustrated. 8vo,   2 00

LIFE OF ST. ALOYSIUS GONZAGA. Edited by Rev. F. GOLDIE, S.J. Edition de luxe, richly illustrated. 8vo,   *net*, 2 50

LIFE OF THE BLESSED VIRGIN, ILLUSTRATED. Adapted by Rev. RICHARD BRENNAN, LL.D. With fine half-tone illustrations. 12mo,   1 25

LIFE OF CHRIST, ILLUSTRATED. By Father M. v. COCHEM. Adapted by Rev. B. HAMMER, O.S.F. With fine half-tone illustrations. 12mo, 1 25

LIFE OF FATHER CHARLES SIRE. By his brother, Rev. VITAL SIRE. 12mo, *net*, 1 00

LIFE OF ST. CLARE OF MONTEFALCO. By Rev. JOSEPH A. LOCKE, O.S.A. 12mo, *net*, 0 75

LIFE OF THE VEN. MARY CRESCENTIA HÖSS. 12mo, *net*, 1 25

LIFE OF ST. FRANCIS SOLANUS. 16mo, *net*, 0 50

LIFE OF ST. GERMAINE COUSIN. 16mo, 0 50

LIFE OF ST. CHANTAL. See under St. CHANTAL. *net*, 4 00

(LIFE OF) MOST REV. JOHN HUGHES, First Archbishop of New York. By Rev. H. A. BRANN, D.D. 12mo, *net*, 0 75

LIFE OF FATHER JOGUES. By Father FELIX MARTIN, S.J. From the French by JOHN GILMARY SHEA. 12mo, *net*, 0 75

LIFE OF MLLE. LE GRAS. 12mo, *net*, 1 25

LIFE OF MARY FOR CHILDREN. By ANNE R. BENNETT, née GLADSTONE. 24mo, illustrated, *net*, 0 50

LIFE OF RIGHT REV. JOHN N. NEUMANN, D.D. By Rev. E. GRIMM, C.SS.R. 12mo, *net*, 1 25

LIFE OF FR. FRANCIS POILVACHE. 32mo, paper, *net*, 0 20

LIFE OF OUR LORD AND SAVIOUR JESUS CHRIST and of His Blessed Mother. Adapted by Rev. RICHARD BRENNAN, LL.D. With nearly 600 illustrations. No. 1. cloth, *net*, 5 00
No. 3. Morocco back and corners, gilt edges, *net*, 7 00
No. 4. Full morocco, richly gilt back, gilt edges, *net*, 9 00
No. 5. Full morocco, block-panelled sides, gilt edges, *net*, 10 00

LIFE, POPULAR, OF ST. TERESA OF JESUS. By L'ABBÉ MARIE-JOSEPH. 12mo, *net*, 0 75

LIGUORI, ST. ALPHONSUS DE. Complete Ascetical Works of. Centenary Edition. Edited by Rev. EUGENE GRIMM, C.SS.R. Price, per volume, *net*, 1 25

Each book is complete in itself, and any volume will be sold separately.

Preparation for Death.
Way of Salvation and of Perfection.
Great Means of Salvation and Perfection.
Incarnation, Birth, and Infancy of Christ.
The Passion and Death of Christ.
The Holy Eucharist.
The Glories of Mary, 2 vols.
Victories of the Martyrs.

True Spouse of Christ, 2 vols.
Dignity and Duties of the Priest.
The Holy Mass.
The Divine Office.
Preaching.
Abridged Sermons for all the Sundays.
Miscellany.
Letters, 4 vols.
Letters and General Index.

LINKED LIVES. A novel. By Lady DOUGLAS. 8vo, 1 50

LITTLE CHILD OF MARY. Large 48mo, 0 25
LITTLE MANUAL OF ST. ANTHONY. Illustrated. 32mo, cloth, 0 60
LITTLE OFFICE OF THE IMMACULATE CONCEPTION. 32mo, paper, 3 cents; per 100, 2 00
LITTLE PICTORIAL LIVES OF THE SAINTS. With Reflections for Every Day in the Year. Edited by JOHN GILMARY SHEA, LL.D. With nearly 400 illustrations. 12mo, cloth, ink and gold side, 1 00
10 copies, 6.25; 25 copies, 15.00; 50 copies, 27.50; 100 copies, 50 00
This book has received the approbation of 30 Archbishops and Bishops.
LITTLE PRAYER-BOOK OF THE SACRED HEART. Prayers and Practices of Blessed Margaret Mary. Sm. 32mo, cloth, 0 40
LITTLE SAINT OF NINE YEARS. From the French of Mgr. DE SEGUR, by MARY MCMAHON. 16mo, 0 50
LOURDES. Its Inhabitants, Its Pilgrims, Its Miracles. By R. F. CLARKE, S.J. 16mo, illustrated, 0 75
LUTHER'S OWN STATEMENTS concerning his Teachings and its Results. By HENRY O'CONNOR, S.J. 12mo, paper, 0 15
MANIFESTATION OF CONSCIENCE. Confessions and Communions in Religious Communities. By Rev. PIE DE LANGOGNE, O.M.Cap. 32mo, *net*, 0 50
MANUAL OF THE HOLY EUCHARIST. Conferences and Pious Practices, with Devotions for Mass, etc. Prepared by Rev. F. X. Lasance, Director of the Tabernacle Society of Cincinnati. Oblong 24mo, 0 75
MANUAL OF THE HOLY FAMILY. Prayers and Instructions for Catholic Parents. 32mo, cloth, 0 60
MANUAL OF INDULGENCED PRAYERS. A Complete Prayer-Book. Arranged and disposed for daily use. Small 32mo, 0 40
MARCELLA GRACE. A novel. By ROSA MULHOLLAND. With illustrations after original drawings. 12mo, 1 25
MARRIAGE. By Very Rev. PÈRE MONSABRÉ, O.P. From the French, by M. HOPPER. 12mo, *net*, 1 00
MAY DEVOTIONS, NEW. Reflections on the Invocations of the Litany of Loretto. 12mo, *net*, 1 00
McCALLEN, REV. JAMES A., S.S. Sanctuary Boy's Illustrated Manual. 12mo, *net*, 0 50
—— Office of Tenebræ. 12mo, *net*, 1 00
—— Appendix. Containing Harmonizations of the Lamentations. 12mo, *net*, 0 75
MEANS OF GRACE, THE. A Complete Exposition of the Seven Sacraments, of the Sacramentals, and of Prayer, with a Comprehensive Explanation of the "Lord's Prayer" and the "Hail Mary." By Rev. RICHARD BRENNAN, LL.D. With 180 full-page and other illustrations. 8vo, cloth, 2.50; gilt edges, 3.00; Library edition, half levant, 3 50
MEDITATIONS (BAXTER) for Every Day in the Year. By Rev. ROGER BAXTER, S.J. Small 12mo, *net*, 1 25

MEDITATIONS (CHAIGNON, S.J.) FOR THE USE OF THE SECULAR CLERGY. By Father CHAIGNON, S.J. From the French, by Rt. Rev. L. DE GOESBRIAND, D.D. 2 vols., 8vo, *net*, 4 00

MEDITATIONS (HAMON'S) FOR ALL THE DAYS OF THE YEAR. For the use of Priests, Religious, and the Laity. By Rev. M. HAMON, SS., Pastor of St. Sulpice, Paris. From the French, by Mrs. ANNE R. BENNETT-GLADSTONE. With Alphabetic Index. 5 vols., 16mo, cloth, gilt top, each with a Steel Engraving. *net*, 5 00

"Hamon's doctrine is the unadulterated word of God, presented with unction, exquisite taste, and freed from that exaggerated and sickly sentimentalism which disgusts when it does not mislead."—MOST REV. P. L. CHAPELLE, D.D.

MEDITATIONS (PERINALDO) on the Sufferings of Jesus Christ. From the Italian of Rev. FRANCIS DA PERINALDO, O.S.F. 12mo, *net*, 0 75

MEDITATIONS (VERCRUYSSE), for Every Day in the Year, on the Life of Our Lord Jesus Christ. By the Rev. Father BRUNO VERCRUYSSE, S.J. 2 vols., *net*, 2 75

MEDITATIONS ON THE PASSION OF OUR LORD. By a PASSIONIST FATHER. 32mo, 0 40

MISSION BOOK of the Redemptorist Fathers. 32mo, cloth, 0 50

MISSION BOOK FOR THE MARRIED. By Very Rev. F. GIRARDEY, C.SS.R. 32mo, 0 50

MISSION BOOK FOR THE SINGLE. By Very Rev. F. GIRARDEY, C.SS.R. 32mo, 0 50

MISTRESS OF NOVICES, The, Instructed in her Duties. From the French of the ABBÉ LEGUAY, by Rev. IGNATIUS SISK. 12mo, cloth, *net*, 0 75

MOMENTS BEFORE THE TABERNACLE. By Rev. MATTHEW RUSSELL, S.J. 24mo, *net*, 0 40

MONK'S PARDON. A Historical Romance of the Time of Philip IV. of Spain. By RAOUL DE NAVERY. 12mo, 1 25

MONTH OF THE DEAD. 32mo, 0 75

MONTH OF MAY. From the French of Father DEBUSSI, S J., by ELLA MCMAHON. 32mo, 0 50

MONTH OF THE SACRED HEART. HUGUET. 0 75

MONTH, NEW, OF MARY, St. Francis de Sales. 32mo, 0 40

MONTH, NEW, OF THE SACRED HEART, St. Francis de Sales. 32mo, 0 40

MONTH, NEW, OF ST. JOSEPH, St. Francis de Sales. 32mo, 0 40

MONTH, NEW, OF THE HOLY ANGELS, St. Francis de Sales. 32mo, 0 40

MOOTED QUESTIONS OF HISTORY. By H. DESMOND. 16mo, 0 75

MR. BILLY BUTTONS. A novel. By WALTER LECKY. 12mo, 1 25

MY FIRST COMMUNION: The Happiest Day of My Life. BRENNAN. 16mo, illustrated, 0 75

MÜLLER, REV. MICHAEL, C.SS.R. God the Teacher of Mankind. A plain, comprehensive Explanation of Christian Doctrine. 9 vols., crown 8vo. Per set, *net*, 9 50
    The Church and Her Enemies. *net*, 1 10
    The Apostles' Creed. *net*, 1 10
    The First and Greatest Commandment. *net*, 1 40
    Explanation of the Commandments, continued. Precepts of the Church. *net*, 1 10
    Dignity, Authority, and Duties of Parents, Ecclesiastical and Civil Powers. Their Enemies. *net*, 1 40
    Grace and the Sacraments. *net*, 1 25
    Holy Mass. *net*, 1 25
    Eucharist and Penance. *net*, 1 10
    Sacramentals—Prayer, etc. *net*, 1 00
—— Familiar Explanation of Catholic Doctrine. 12mo, 1 00
—— The Prodigal Son; or, The Sinner's Return to God. 8vo, *net*, 1 00
—— The Devotion of the Holy Rosary and the Five Scapulars. 8vo, *net*, 0 75
—— The Catholic Priesthood. 2 vols., 8vo, *net*, 3 00

NAMES THAT LIVE IN CATHOLIC HEARTS. By ANNA T. SADLIER. 12mo, 1 00

NEW TESTAMENT, THE. Illustrated Edition. With 100 fine full-page illustrations. Printed in two colors. 16mo, *net*, 0 60

The advantages of this edition over others consist in its beautiful illustrations, its convenient size, its clear, open type, and substantial and attractive binding. It is the best adapted for general use on account of its compactness and low price.

OFFICE, COMPLETE, OF HOLY WEEK, in Latin and English. 24mo, cloth, 0.50; cloth, limp, gilt edges, 1 00
    Also in finer bindings.

O'GRADY, ELEANOR. Aids to Correct and Effective Elocution. 12mo, 1 25
—— Select Recitations for Schools and Academies. 12mo, 1 00
—— Readings and Recitations for Juniors. 16mo, *net*, 0 50
—— Elocution Class. 16mo, *net*, 0 50

ON CHRISTIAN ART. By EDITH HEALY. 16mo, 0 50

ON THE ROAD TO ROME, and How Two Brothers Got There. By WILLIAM RICHARDS. 16mo, 0 50

ONE AND THIRTY DAYS WITH BLESSED MARGARET MARY. 32mo, flexible cloth, 0 25

ONE ANGEL MORE IN HEAVEN. With Letters of Condolence by St. Francis de Sales and others. White mor., 0 50

OUR BIRTHDAY BOUQUET. Culled from the Shrines of Saints and the Gardens of Poets. By E. C. DONNELLY. 16mo, 1 00

OUR FAVORITE DEVOTIONS. By Very Rev. Dean A. A. LINGS. 24mo, 0 60

While there are many excellent books of devotion, there is none made on the plans of this one, giving ALL the devotions in general use among the faithful. It will be found a very serviceable book.

OUR FAVORITE NOVENAS. By the Very Rev. Dean A. A.
 LINGS. 24mo, 0 60
 Gives forms of prayer for all the novenas for the feasts of Our Lord, the Blessed Virgin, and the Saints which pious custom has established.
OUR LADY OF GOOD COUNSEL IN GENAZZANO. By
 ANNE R. BENNETT, née GLADSTONE. 32mo, 0 75
OUR OWN WILL, and How to Detect it in our Actions. By Rev.
 JOHN ALLEN, D.D. 16mo, net, 0 75
OUR YOUNG FOLKS' LIBRARY. 10 volumes. 12mo. Each,
 0 45; per set, 3 00
OUTLAW OF CAMARGUE, THE. A novel. By A. DE LAMOTHE,
 12mo, 1 25
OUTLINES OF DOGMATIC THEOLOGY. By Rev. SYLVESTER
 J. HUNTER, S.J. 3 vols., 12mo, net, 4 50
PARADISE ON EARTH OPENED TO ALL; or, A Religious
 Vocation the Surest Way in Life. 32mo, net, 0 40
PASSING SHADOWS. A novel. By ANTHONY YORKE. 12mo, 1 25
PEARLS FROM FABER. Selected and arranged by MARION J.
 BRUNOWE. 32mo, 0 50
PETRONILLA, and other Stories. By E. C. DONNELLY. 12mo, 1 00
PHILOSOPHY, ENGLISH MANUALS OF CATHOLIC.
    Logic. By RICHARD F. CLARKE, S.J. 12mo, net, 1 25
    First Principles of Knowledge. By JOHN RICKABY, S.J.
 12mo, net, 1 25
    Moral Philosophy (Ethics and Natural Law). By JOSEPH
 RICKABY, S.J. 12mo, net, 1 25
    Natural Theology. By BERNARD BOEDDER, S.J. 12mo, net, 1 50
    Psychology. By MICHAEL MAHER, S.J. 12mo, net, 1 50
    General Metaphysics. By JOHN RICKABY, S.J. 12mo, net, 1 25
    Manual of Political Economy. By C. S. DEVAS. 12mo, net, 1 50
PEW-RENT RECEIPT BOOK. 800 receipts, net, 1 00
PICTORIAL LIVES OF THE SAINTS. With Reflections for
 Every Day in the Year. 50th Thousand. 8vo. 2 00
 5 copies, 6.65; 10 copies, 12.50; 25 copies, 27.50; 50 copies, 50 00
POPULAR INSTRUCTIONS ON MARRIAGE. By Very Rev.
 F. GIRARDEY, C.SS.R. 32mo. Paper, 0.25; per 100, 12 50
 Cloth, 0.35; per 100, 21 00
POPULAR INSTRUCTIONS TO PARENTS on the Bringing Up
 of Children. By Very Rev. F. GIRARDEY, C.SS.R. 32mo.
 Paper, 0.25; per 100, 12.50. Cloth, 0.35; per 100, 21 00
PRAYER. The Great Means of Obtaining Salvation. LIGUORI.
 32mo, 0 50
PRAYER-BOOK FOR LENT. Meditations and Prayers for Lent.
 32mo, cloth, 0 50
PRAXIS SYNODALIS. Manuale Synodi Diocesanæ ac Provin-
 cialis Celebrandæ. 12mo, net, 0 60
PRIEST IN THE PULPIT, THE. A Manual of Homiletics and
 Catechetics. SCHUECH-LUEBBERMANN. 8vo, net, 1 50
PRIMER FOR CONVERTS, A. By Rev. J. T. DURWARD. 32mo,
 flexible cloth, 0 25

PRINCIPLES OF ANTHROPOLOGY AND BIOLOGY. By Rev.
THOMAS HUGHES, S.J. 16mo, *net*, 0 75

REASONABLENESS OF CATHOLIC CEREMONIES AND
PRACTICES. By Rev. J. J. BURKE. 12mo, flexible cloth, 0 35

READING AND THE MIND, WITH SOMETHING TO READ.
O'CONOR, S.J. 12mo, *net*, 0 50

REGISTRUM BAPTISMORUM. 3,200 registers. 11 x 16
inches, *net*, 3 50

REGISTRUM MATRIMONIORUM. 3,200 registers. 11 x 16
inches, *net*, 3 50

RELIGIOUS STATE, THE. With a Short Treatise on Vocation
to the Priesthood. By ST. ALPHONSUS LIGUORI. 32mo, 0 50

REMINISCENCES OF RT. REV. EDGAR P. WADHAMS, D.D.,
By Rev. C. A. WALWORTH. 12mo, illustrated, *net*, 1 00

RIGHTS OF OUR LITTLE ONES; or, First Principles of Education in Catechetical Form. By Rev. JAMES CONWAY, S.J.
32mo, paper, 0.15; per 100, 9.00; cloth, 0.25; per 100, 15 00

ROSARY, THE MOST HOLY, in Thirty-one Meditations, Prayers,
and Examples. By Rev. EUGENE GRIMM, C.SS.R. 32mo, 0 50

ROUND TABLE, A, of the Representative *American* Catholic
Novelists, containing the best stories by the best writers. With
half-tone portraits, printed in colors, biographical sketches, etc.
12mo, 1 50

ROUND TABLE, A, of the Representative *Irish and English*
Catholic Novelists, containing the best stories by the best
writers. With half-tone portraits, printed in colors, biographical
sketches, etc. 12mo, 1 50

RUSSO, N., S.J.—De Philosophia Morali Prælectiones in Collegio
Georgiopolitano Soc. Jes. Anno 1889-1890 Habitæ, a Patre
NICOLAO RUSSO. Editio altera. 8vo, half leather, *net*, 2 00

SACRAMENT OF PENANCE, THE. Lenten Sermons. Paper,
net, 0 25

SACRIFICE OF THE MASS WORTHILY CELEBRATED, THE.
By the Rev. Father CHAIGNON, S.J. Translated by Rt. Rev. L.
DE GOESBRIAND, D.D. 8vo, *net*, 1 50

SACRISTY RITUAL. Rituale Compendiosum, seu Ordo Administrandi quædam Sacramenta et alia officia Ecclesiastica Rite peragendi ex Rituale Romano novissime edito desumptas. 16mo,
flexible, *net*, 0 75

ST. CHANTAL AND THE FOUNDATION OF THE VISITATION. By Monseigneur BOUGAUD. 2 vols., 8vo, *net*, 4 00

ST. JOSEPH OUR ADVOCATE. From the French of Rev. Father
HUGUET. 24mo, 1 00

SACRAMENTALS OF THE HOLY CATHOLIC CHURCH,
THE. By Rev. A. A. LAMBING, LL.D. Illustrated edition.
24mo.
    Paper, 0.25; 25 copies, 4.25; 50 copies, 7.50; 100 copies, 12 50
    Cloth, 0.50; 25 copies, 8.50; 50 copies, 15.00; 100 copies, 25 00

SACRED HEART, BOOKS ON THE.
    Child's Prayer-Book of the Sacred Heart. Small 32mo,   0 25
    Devotions to the Sacred Heart for the First Friday. 32mo, 0 40
    Imitation of the Sacred Heart of Jesus. By Rev. F. ARNOUDT, S.J. From the Latin by Rev. J. M. FASTRE, S.J. 16mo, cloth, 1 25
    Little Prayer-Book of the Sacred Heart. Small 32mo,   0 40
    Month of the Sacred Heart of Jesus. HUGUET. 32mo,   0 75
    Month of the Sacred Heart for the Young Christian. By BROTHER PHILIPPE. 32mo,   0 50
    New Month of the Sacred Heart, St. Francis de Sales. 32mo, 0 40
    One and Thirty Days with Blessed Margaret Mary. 32mo, 0 25
    Pearls from the Casket of the Sacred Heart of Jesus. 32mo, 0 50
    Revelations of the Sacred Heart to Blessed Margaret Mary; and the History of her Life. BOUGAUD. 8vo, *net*, 1 50
    Sacred Heart Studied in the Sacred Scriptures. By Rev. H. SAINTRAIN, C.SS.R. 8vo, *net*, 2 00
    Six Sermons on Devotion to the Sacred Heart of Jesus. BIERBAUM. 16mo, *net*, 0 60
    Year of the Sacred Heart. Drawn from the works of PÈRE DE LA COLOMBIÈRE, of Margaret Mary, and of others. 32mo, 0 50

SACRED RHETORIC. 12mo, *net*, 0 75

SECRET OF SANCTITY, THE. According to ST. FRANCIS DE SALES and Father CRASSET, S.J. 12mo, *net*, 1 00

SERAPHIC GUIDE. A Manual for the Members of the Third Order of St. Francis.   0 60
    Roan, red edges,   0 75
    The same in German at the same prices.

SERMONS. See also "Sacrament of Penance," "Seven Last Words," "Two-Edged Sword," and "Hunolt."

SERMONS, EIGHT SHORT PRACTICAL, ON MIXED MARRIAGES. By Rev. A. A. LAMBING, LL.D. Paper, *net*, 0 25

SERMONS, OLD AND NEW. 8 vols., 8vo, *net*, 16 00

SERMONS, LENTEN. Large 8vo, *net*, 2 00

SERMONS, FUNERAL. 2 vols., *net*, 2 00

SERMONS ON THE CHRISTIAN VIRTUES. By the Rev. F. HUNOLT, S.J. Translated by Rev. J. ALLEN, D.D. 2 vols., 8vo, *net*, 5 00

SERMONS ON THE DIFFERENT STATES OF LIFE. By Rev. F. HUNOLT, S.J. Translated by Rev. J. ALLEN, D.D. 2 vols., 8vo, *net*, 5 00

SERMONS ON THE SEVEN DEADLY SINS. By Rev. F. HUNOLT, S.J. Translated by Rev. J. ALLEN, D.D. 2 vols., 8vo., *net*, 5 00

SERMONS ON PENANCE. By Rev. F. HUNOLT, S.J. Translated by Rev. J. ALLEN, D.D. 2 vols., 8vo, *net*, 5 00

SERMONS ON OUR LORD, THE BLESSED VIRGIN, AND THE SAINTS. By Rev. F. HUNOLT, S.J. Translated by Rev. J. ALLEN, D.D. 2 vols., 8vo, *net*, 5 00

SERMONS ON THE BLESSED VIRGIN. By Very Rev. D. I. MCDERMOTT. 16mo, *net*, 0 75

SERMONS, abridged, for all the Sundays and Holydays. By ST. ALPHONSUS LIGUORI. 12mo, *net*, 1 25

SERMONS for the Sundays and Chief Festivals of the Ecclesiastical Year. With Two Courses of Lenten Sermons and a Triduum for the Forty Hours. By Rev. JULIUS POTTGEISSER, S.J. From the German by Rev. JAMES CONWAY, S.J. 2 vols., 8vo, *net*, 2 50

SERMONS ON THE MOST HOLY ROSARY. By Rev. M. J. FRINGS. 12mo, *net*, 1 00

SERMONS, SHORT, FOR LOW MASSES. A complete, brief course of instruction on Christian Doctrine. By Rev. F. X. SCHOUPPE, S.J. 12mo, *net*, 1 25

SERMONS, SIX, on Devotion to the Sacred Heart of Jesus. From the German of Rev. Dr. E. BIERBAUM, by ELLA MCMAHON, 16mo, *net*, 0 60

SEVEN LAST WORDS ON THE CROSS. Sermons. Paper, *net*, 0 25

SHORT CONFERENCES ON THE LITTLE OFFICE OF THE IMMACULATE CONCEPTION. By Very Rev. JOSEPH RAINER. With Prayers. 32mo, 0 50

SHORT STORIES ON CHRISTIAN DOCTRINE: A Collection of Examples Illustrating the Catechism. From the French by MARY MCMAHON. 12mo, illustrated, *net*, 0 75

SMITH, Rev. S. B., D.D. Elements of Ecclesiastical Law.
    Vol. I. Ecclesiastical Persons. 8vo, *net*, 2 50
    Vol. II. Ecclesiastical Trials. 8vo, *net*, 2 50
    Vol. III. Ecclesiastical Punishments. 8vo, *net*, 2 50

———— Compendium Juris Canonici, ad Usum Cleri et Seminariorum hujus regionis accommodatum. 8vo, *net*, 2 00

———— The Marriage Process in the United States. 8vo, *net*, 2 50

SODALISTS' VADE MECUM. A Manual, Prayer-Book, and Hymnal. 32mo, cloth, 0 50

SOUVENIR OF THE NOVITIATE. From the French by Rev. EDWARD I. TAYLOR. 32mo, *net*, 0 60

SPIRITUAL CRUMBS FOR HUNGRY LITTLE SOULS. To which are added Stories from the Bible. RICHARDSON. 16mo, 0 50

STANG, Rev. WILLIAM, D.D. Pastoral Theology. New enlarged edition. 8vo, *net*, 1 50

———— Eve of the Reformation. 12mo, paper, *net*, 0 50

STORIES FOR FIRST COMMUNICANTS, for the Time before and after First Communion. By Rev. J. A. KELLER, D.D. 32mo, 0 50

SUMMER AT WOODVILLE, A. By ANNA T. SADLIER. 16mo, 0 50

SURE WAY TO A HAPPY MARRIAGE. A Book of Instructions for those Betrothed and for Married People. From the German by Rev. Edward I. Taylor. Paper, 0.25; per 100, 12.50; cloth, 0.35; per 100, 21 00

TALES AND LEGENDS OF THE MIDDLE AGES. From the Spanish of F. De P. Capella. By Henry Wilson. 16mo, 0 75

TAMING OF POLLY, THE. By Ella Loraine Dorsey. 12mo, 0 85

TANQUEREY, Rev. Ad., S.S. Synopsis Theologiæ Fundamentalis. 8vo, *net*, 1 50

—— Synopsis Theologia Dogmatica Specialis. 2 vols., 8vo, *net*, 3 00

THINK WELL ON'T; or, Reflections on the Great Truths of the Christian Religion. By the Right Rev. R. Challoner, D.D. 32mo, flexible cloth, 0 20

THOUGHT FROM ST. ALPHONSUS, for Every Day of the Year. 32mo, 0 50

THOUGHT FROM BENEDICTINE SAINTS. 32mo, 0 50

THOUGHT FROM DOMINICAN SAINTS. 32mo, 0 50

THOUGHT FROM ST. FRANCIS ASSISI and his Saints. 32mo, 0 50

THOUGHT FROM ST. IGNATIUS. 32mo, 0 50

THOUGHT FROM ST. TERESA. 32mo, 0 50

THOUGHT FROM ST. VINCENT DE PAUL. 32mo, 0 50

THOUGHTS AND COUNSELS FOR THE CONSIDERATION OF CATHOLIC YOUNG MEN. By Rev. P. A. Von Doss, S.J. 12mo, *net*, 1 25

THREE GIRLS AND ESPECIALLY ONE. By Marion Ames Taggart. 16mo, 0 50

TRUE POLITENESS. Addressed to Religious. By Rev. Francis Demare. 16mo, *net*, 0 60

TRUE SPOUSE OF CHRIST. By St. Alphonsus Liguori. 2 vols., 12mo, *net*, 2.50; 1 vol., 12mo, 1 50

TWELVE VIRTUES, THE, of a Good Teacher. For Mothers, Instructors, etc. By Rev. H. Pottier, S.J. 32mo, *net*, 0 30

TWO-EDGED SWORD, THE. Lenten Sermons. Paper. *net*, 0 25

TWO RETREATS FOR SISTERS. By Rev. E. Zollner. 12mo, *net*, 1 00

VADE MECUM SACERDOTUM. Continens Preces ante et post Missam modum providendi Infirmos nec non multas Benedictionum Formulas. 48mo, cloth, *net*, 0.25; morocco, flexible, *net*, 0 50

VISIT TO EUROPE AND THE HOLY LAND. By Rev. H. F. Fairbanks. 12mo, illustrated, 1 50

VISITS TO THE MOST HOLY SACRAMENT and to the Blessed Virgin Mary. For Every Day of the Month. By St. Alphonsus de Liguori. Edited by Rev. Eugene Grimm. 32mo, 0 50

VOCATIONS EXPLAINED: Matrimony, Virginity, the Religious State, and the Priesthood. By a Vincentian Father. 16mo, flexible, 10 cents; per 100, 5 00

WARD, REV. THOS. F. Fifty-two Instructions on the Principal Truths of Our Holy Religion. 12mo, *net*, 0 75

—— Thirty-two Instructions for the Month of May and for the Feasts of the Blessed Virgin. 12mo, *net*, 0 75

—— Month of May at Mary's Altar. 12mo, *net*, 0 75

—— Short Instructions for all the Sundays and Holydays. 12mo, *net*, 1 25

WAY OF INTERIOR PEACE. By Rev. Father DE LEHEN, S.J. From the German Version of Rev. J. BRUCKER, S.J. 12mo, *net*, 1 25

WAY OF THE CROSS. Illustrated. Paper, 5 cents; per 100, 3 00

WHAT CATHOLICS HAVE DONE FOR SCIENCE, with Sketches of the Great Catholic Scientists. By Rev. MARTIN S. BRENNAN. 12mo, 1 00

WOMAN OF FORTUNE, A. A novel. By CHRISTIAN REID. 12mo, 1 25

WOMEN OF CATHOLICITY: Margaret O'Carroll—Isabella of Castile—Margaret Roper—Marie de l'Incarnation—Margaret Bourgeoys—Ethan Allen's Daughter. By ANNA T. SADLIER. 12mo, 1 00

WORDS OF JESUS CHRIST DURING HIS PASSION, Explained in their Literal and Moral Sense. By Rev. F. X. SCHOUPPE, S.J. Flexible cloth, 0 25

WORDS OF WISDOM. A Concordance of the Sapiential Books. 12mo, *net*, 1 25

WUEST, REV. JOSEPH, C.SS.R. DEVOTIO QUADRAGINTA HORARUM. 32mo, *net*, 0 25

YOUNG GIRL'S BOOK OF PIETY. 16mo, 1 00

ZEAL IN THE WORK OF THE MINISTRY; or, The Means by which every Priest may render his Ministry Honorable and Fruitful. From the French of L'ABBÉ DUBOIS. 8vo, *net*, 1 50

AN AMERICAN INDUSTRY. A full description of the Silversmith's Art and Ecclesiastical Metalwork as carried on in Benziger Brothers' Factory of Church Goods, De Kalb Avenue and Rockwell Place, Brooklyn, N. Y. Small quarto, 48 pp., with 75 illustrations, printed in two colors. Mailed gratis on application.

This interesting book gives a full description of the various arts employed in the manufacture of Church goods, from the designing and modelling, through the different branches of casting, spinning, chasing, buffing, gilding, and burnishing. The numerous beautiful half-tone illustrations show the machinery and tools used, as well as rich specimens of the work turned out.

www.ingramcontent.com/pod-product-compliance
Lightning Source LLC
Chambersburg PA
CBHW031831230426
43669CB00009B/1302